JOSEPH

A Life of Virtue

W. ROSS RAINEY

Developed as a study course by Emmaus Correspondence School, founded in 1942.

ECS Ministries exists to glorify God by providing doctrinally-sound resources and structured study materials for the purpose of teaching people from every nation to know Jesus Christ as Savior and to live in a way that is consistent with God's Word.

Joseph: A Life of Virtue

W. Ross Rainey

Published by:

Emmaus Correspondence School
(A division of ECS Ministries)
PO Box 1028
Dubuque, IA 52004-1028
phone: (563) 585-2070
email: ecsorders@emmauscourses.org
website: www.emmauscourses.org

Many Bible study courses may also be taken via smart phones, tablets, and computers. For more information, visit: www.emmauscourses.org.

First Printed 2010 (AK '10), 1 Unit
Reprinted 2012 (AK '10), 1 Unit
Reprinted 2017 (AK '10), 1 Unit

ISBN 978-1-59387-109-3

Code: JOS

Printed in the United States of America

COURSE OVERVIEW

The life of Joseph is a classic Old Testament illustration of the biblical principle that "all things work together for good to them that love God, to them who are the called according to His purpose" (Rom. 8:28). We can rest assured that God allows the trials of life to teach us things we would not otherwise learn. The believer's life is not always a picnic. We need to learn to trust God, this being a primary reason for such trials, keeping in mind that God's preeminent and overall purpose is to conform us increasingly into the image of Christ Jesus, His Son (Rom. 8:29).

Lessons You Will Study

STUDENT INSTRUCTIONS

How to Study

This course has two parts—the lesson content and the exam booklet. Before you begin to study, ask God to open your heart so that you can receive the truths that He wants to teach you from His Word. The study of the Bible brings great discoveries and bears rich fruit in the life of a believer. The following study guidelines will be helpful in order to gain the most from this course.

Read each chapter through at least twice, once to get a general idea of its content and then again, slowly, looking up any Bible references given. It is important that you read the Bible passages referenced as some questions may be based on the Bible text. We suggest that you keep a regular schedule by trying to complete at least one chapter per week.

Exams

At the end of the course there is an exam booklet with one exam for each lesson. (If a Single Page Answer Sheet is also included, **carefully read all instructions** and completely fill it out before mailing it in for grading.) Do not answer the questions by what you think or have always believed. The questions are designed to find out if you understand the material in the course.

At the end of each exam, there is a *What Do You Say?* question. These questions are included for your own reflection. They will not be counted as part of your grade, but instead provide an opportunity for you to personally meditate on the lesson.

Getting Exams Graded

When you have answered all the exam questions, fill in your contact information and mail it back to the instructor, associated ministry, or organization from which you received it. After finishing this course with a passing average, you will be awarded a certificate.

We are excited to be a part of your study of God's Word. May the Lord bless your study of His Word with joy and fruitfulness!

CHAPTER

1

JOSEPH, BELOVED AND HATED
(GENESIS 37:1-17)

Introduction

Joseph is one of the most endearing and outstanding characters in the Bible, and the study of his life offers many practical lessons for believers today.

The first reference to Joseph's life is in Genesis 37:2. However, his birth and references to his name are recorded in Genesis 30:24 and 25; 33:2 and 7, and 35:24. Joseph was the eleventh son of Jacob and the first child of Rachel, Jacob's second and favorite wife. He was born into a family

> More chapters in Genesis are devoted to Joseph than to any other person.

which had many failures, including polygamy, favoritism, rape, murder, incest, and prostitution. Yet, in spite of this sordid background, Joseph stands out as one of the most beautiful characters in the Bible. More chapters in Genesis are devoted to him than to any other person, including Abraham. Like Daniel, not one negative thing is recorded against Joseph. This does not mean that these men were not sinners, but that it was God's purpose to not record any of their faults and failures.

Of all the Hebrew characters in the Old Testament, Joseph is the most perfect example of the Lord Jesus Christ. However, nowhere in the New Testament is he specifically mentioned as a type (picture) of Christ. While heredity and environment influence all of us, Joseph is an excellent example of someone who lived a godly life. He refused to follow the sinful lifestyle of his wayward brothers or allow the general corruption of his day to tempt him to sin.

5

W. H. Griffith Thomas, the well-known British Bible teacher and author, has commented on the value and importance of the story of Joseph from a fourfold standpoint: (1) it throws light on divine providence; (2) it supplies the reader with important historical information about the Hebrews; (3) it gives a splendid example of personal character in its portrayal of this man Joseph; and (4) it provides a striking series of pictures of the Lord Jesus Christ.

The record of Joseph is part of a much larger purpose of God. When God confirmed His covenant with Abraham, He said, "Know certainly that your descendants will be strangers in a land that is not theirs, and will serve them, and they will afflict them four hundred years" (Gen. 15:13). This refers, of course, to Israel's bondage in Egypt. God's method of getting the descendants of Abraham (Jacob's family) to Egypt was through Joseph's experiences.

The widely known Scottish preacher and author, W. Graham Scroggie, summed up Joseph's life as follows: "We see him in three aspects: first, as the princely son; second, as the patient sufferer; and third, as the people's savior."

In our Scripture passage of Genesis 37:1-17, two main things are drawn to our attention regarding Joseph, the first being that he was loved by his father.

Loved by His Father (37:1-3)

Genesis 36, which concerns the generations of Esau, is something of a parenthesis in the overall story of Joseph's life. Through all of these background details and events, God was preparing for the transformation of the household and the tribe into a nation.

The account opens when Joseph was seventeen years old (v. 2), always an age of great importance in a young person's life. We also note from verse 2 that Joseph was shepherding the flock with his brothers. The sons with whom he was particularly associated were Bilhah's sons, Dan and Naphtali (30:5-7), and Zilpah's sons, Gad and Asher (30:9-13).

Joseph brought a "bad report" of his brothers to Jacob. Exactly what the bad report was about we don't know. Nor do we know whether Joseph's action was right or wrong. His first responsibility was to his father, and in this light he acted properly. It may be that Joseph brought in the report about his brothers because he was ashamed that God's name was being blasphemed among the inhabitants of the land. Or it may be that he was simply concerned for the family name which had been disgraced (cf. 34:30).

Jacob loved Joseph more than all his children because he was the son of his old age (vv. 3-4), and probably because he was Rachel's son.* Jacob's own experience of favoritism in his youth seems to have taught him nothing (Genesis 27). He doted on Joseph and showed his favoritism by giving him "a tunic of many colors." This gesture marked him out as superior, expressing Jacob's intention to make him preeminent above his brothers. A similar garment is described in 2 Samuel 13:18, a dress of Tamar, King David's daughter, thus referring to royal apparel. We are not surprised at the way Joseph's brothers reacted. This brings us to the second main point in our Scripture passage—namely, the fact that Joseph was hated by his brothers.

Hated by His Brothers (37:4-17)

Why did Joseph's brothers hate him? Three reasons are given: (1) because of his evil report of them; (2) because of his father's favoritism; and (3) because of his dreams. For all this they hated him with a growing hatred (see vv. 2, 4, 5, 8).

At this point we need to focus on two things, the first being *Joseph's revelation of his dreams*. Joseph was already hated (v. 4). Now his brothers' hatred of him was further fueled by the two dreams he had that were related to each other. The first dream clearly affirmed that Joseph was to have the right to rule over his brothers. The second dream affirmed his supremacy over the entire family. Jacob had no problem understanding the meaning of this second dream (cf. v. 10).

The second thing we note is *the family's reaction to his dreams*. Joseph's brothers not only hated him; now they were envious of him. However, Jacob

---

* In his commentary on Genesis, Ken Fleming writes: "His [Joseph's] moral and spiritual standards were obviously higher than the others. He was called 'the son of his old age,' meaning he was a 'wise son.' In our idiom, we would say he was mature for his age. The phrase does not mean there was a large age gap between him and his older brothers; all eleven had been born in a seven-year period (Gen. 29:30-31:24)." Ken Fleming, *Genesis: From Creation to a Nation*, (Dubuque, IA: ECS Ministries, 2005) 343.

reminds us of Mary, the mother of Jesus. When she heard things about her infant son, she "kept all these things and pondered them in her heart" (Luke 2:19). Jacob began to suspect that some divine purpose was involved in Joseph's unusual dreams.

Evidently Jacob was anxious about his sons who were shepherding the flock at Shechem, where they had already disgraced his name (cf. 34:30). He therefore sent Joseph to check on them. Joseph immediately obeyed his father and traveled from Hebron to Shechem, about 50 miles away. He failed to find his brothers there, but with the help of a stranger he eventually located them at Dothan, another 15 miles away.

> Only the grace of God in one's heart and life is truly able to overcome the sin of envy.

Joseph was quick to obey his father. The disobedience of children to their parents is a sure sign of the fragmenting of families. Children can affect the emotional life of their parents. Proverbs 10:1 says, "A wise son makes a glad father, but a foolish son is the grief of his mother."

POINTS TO PONDER

1. Among other things, it clearly illustrates the sin of man and the grace of God, the sin of envy being particularly stressed (cf. Psalm 37:1; 73:3; Romans 13:13). Envy is "the rottenness of the bones" (Prov. 14:30; see James 3:16), and there can be no peace when it is present. It is the root of many of our sins against others. Remember, it was for "envy" that the chief priests and elders of Israel delivered the Lord Jesus Christ to Pilate to be tried (Matt. 27:18). If God were first in our lives, there would be no envy (see Psalm 37:3-7 and 1 Corinthians 13:4). Only the grace of God in one's heart and life is truly able to overcome this sin.

   Envy is defined as "a feeling of discontentment and resentment aroused by contemplation of another's possessions, qualities, or achievements, with a strong wish that they were one's own." Some may think of envy and jealousy as interchangeable terms, but there is a distinction between the two words.

   "Envy consists largely of unhappiness over the success of others; in fact, it may even rejoice in the failure of others.

Jealousy, on the other hand, is the pain of losing what we have to someone else. Jealousy may even begin in love—a love so intense that any disruption of that love is met with violence. Jealousy has been defined as the torture of loving that which one no longer has the power to possess."

–John D. Jess

Envy leads to anger, hatred, and even murder. There are many classic examples of it in the Bible. Consider the following: Cain's anger and murder of his brother Abel (Gen. 4:4-8); Sarah's envy of her handmaid Hagar which brought strife and division into Abraham's family (Gen. 16:5-6; 21:9, 10); King Saul's envy of David's growing popularity (1 Sam. 18:8-9, 29; 20:31); Haman's envy of Mordecai sitting at the king's gate (Esther 5:13); the Babylonian princes' envy of Daniel's faultless character (Dan. 6:4); the Jews' envy of the success of Paul and Barnabas's ministry (Acts 13:45-50); and likewise of Paul and Silas's ministry (Acts 17:1-9).

2. Another lesson we learn from Genesis 37 is the harm done to a family when one parent or the other favors a particular child. Rebekah's favor of Jacob over Esau led her to trick her husband Isaac into giving Esau's birthright to Jacob (Gen. 27:1-40). As a result, Jacob had to flee for his life. Sadly, the home was broken up and Rebekah never saw her son Jacob again. Unfortunately, sin has a way of repeating itself from one generation to another (see Exodus 20:5 and Numbers 14:18), as illustrated by Jacob being deceived by *his* sons (that we shall soon see).

> **Just because someone comes from a divided home does not mean that he or she cannot become a godly person.**

It cannot be denied that environment has a big influence on the direction of one's life. However, all too often it is used as an excuse for one's sin and failure. Joseph came from a rough background, especially when we think of the unsavory character of his brothers. Nevertheless, he became one of the most godly examples we have record of in the Old Testament. Just because someone comes from a divided home, perhaps with a background of alcoholism or drug abuse, does not mean that he or she cannot become a godly person. Many have suffered physical, sexual, verbal, or psychological abuse who have, by God's grace and His good hand, overcome such obstacles and gone on to live productive and Christ-honoring lives. Have you allowed God's grace to give you the victory over problems of your past, whether they be a divided home, hatred, envy, or some kind of abuse?

2

SOLD INTO EGYPT
(GENESIS 37:18-36)

Consider this comment about Joseph's brothers from the 20th century preacher Donald Grey Barnhouse:

"They had hated Joseph for a long time, even as man's enmity against God burned from the beginning. 'The carnal mind is enmity against God' (Romans 8:7), and this enmity will continue to the end . . . it will be the same story to the end, when the inhabitants of the world encamp against the holy city (Revelation 20:9). Man's hatred of God and of the Lord Jesus Christ is the strangest fact of history. It reveals how far the fall took men from God, and how terrible the Adamic heart really is."

Four main themes come before us in this second half of Genesis 37: the scheming of Joseph's brothers, the strategy of Rueben, the selling of Joseph, and the sorrow of Jacob.

> Man's hatred of God and of the Lord Jesus Christ reveals how far the fall took men from God.

The Scheming of Joseph's Brothers (37:18-20)

The brothers recognized Joseph from a distance, perhaps by his walk or his clothes. Mockingly speaking of him as "this dreamer" (literally, "master of dreams"), they launched into a series of schemes, desiring to kill him and throw his body into one of the many artificial cisterns that were nearby for the collection of rainwater. They were prepared to lie and say that wild beasts had devoured him. They were evidently annoyed by Joseph's dreams for they said, "We shall see what will become of his dreams!"

The Strategy of Reuben (37:21-22)

> "The intervention of Reuben is remarkable, in view of the fact that he had lost the birthright to Joseph. 'He delivered him out of their hands,' would indicate that he used force to keep his bloodthirsty brothers from murdering Joseph"
>
> –Barnhouse

Reuben was the firstborn son, and therefore the more answerable among his brothers for whatever happened to Joseph. Since blood (especially a brother's, see Genesis 4:10; 9:5b) was sacred, and the fact that he (Rueben) was already out of his father's favor, he knew that what he did with Joseph could either make or break him. Thus he suggested that no blood be shed, but that Joseph be thrown in a pit. His strategy was that he would return later to rescue him and send him home to his father.

> "In making this proposition he did a good thing, but not the best; he sacrificed a measure of principle in the interests of policy; he prevented a deadly wrong, without defending the right; and then, significantly enough, he disappeared, for he was not present when Joseph was sold [Genesis 37:29]. Imperfect goodness is true of us all."
>
> –Scroggie

How do we account for descendants of the noble and godly Abraham behaving so sinfully? One answer is that they were also the sons of Adam, and they simply manifested the depravity in the whole of their being. Also, they were the product of a bigamous home, a home lacking the love, harmony, and discipline that generally come from a monogamous one in keeping with divine principles and where parents listen to, heed, and teach the Word of God.

The Selling of Joseph (37:23-28)

When Joseph reached his brothers they immediately stripped him of his tunic. Probably the very sight of it reminded them of their father's favoritism. An added detail of the hardness of the hearts of Joseph's brothers is revealed in verse 25. While Joseph was crying for mercy in the pit (see 42:21) "they sat down to eat." The prophet Amos referred to this event when he wrote of those "who drink wine from bowls, and anoint yourselves with the best ointments, but are not grieved for the affliction of Joseph" (Amos 6:6).

The brothers' hatred of Joseph blinded them to human decency. Cruelty is a natural outflow of envy and bitterness toward another person. Joseph, a young man of seventeen, must have been terrified.

It was at this point that a caravan of Ishmaelites from Gilead appeared. It bore the spices of that land (see Jeremiah 8:22) and other items that the Egyptians sought for embalming and medicinal purposes. It should be noted that *Ishmaelites* and *Midianites* are interchangeable terms, Abraham having been the one ancestor (see Genesis 16:15; 25:2; and Judges 8:24).

Judah was the next of Joseph's brothers to speak up, and in place of slaying Joseph he proposed slavery (vv. 26-27). In the final analysis it was Judah who prevented Joseph being murdered. So Joseph was sold for twenty pieces of silver. Under the law established at Mt. Sinai with the nation of Israel many hundreds of years later, this was the price fixed for a male slave between five and twenty years old (Lev. 27:5).

The Sorrow of Jacob (37:29-36)

Reuben was away when Joseph was sold—just why and where we don't know. Upon his return to the pit he was absolutely devastated (v. 29). He then returned to his brothers in an agitated state (v. 30).

It has been observed from the details of this passage of Scripture that no sin stands alone. Each needs another to support it. Unkindness calls in the aid of untruth (vv. 31-32). Joseph's brothers did not merely speak the lie to their father, they acted it (Scroggie).

The goat's blood has a certain irony about it (cf. 27:9). Isaac and Rebekah were Jacob's father and mother. Rebekah deceived her husband by means of skins of the kids of a goat. The detailed account of Rebekah's deception and some of the sad consequences are found in Genesis 27. At any rate, if Jacob had been able to control his grief, he might have questioned why Joseph's coat was not torn but only stained by blood. For the time being, everything worked out beautifully for these brutal brothers, but don't ever forget the truth of Numbers 32:23b: "Be sure your sin will find you out." Or, as has often been stated, "Be sure your sin will find you ouch!"

The chapter closes by letting us know that Joseph reached Egypt and was sold to Potiphar, the captain of Pharaoh's bodyguard.

POINTS TO PONDER

1. As we think about Jacob's reaction to trouble (vv. 33-35), we do well to think of the different attitudes people have in a time of trouble. Trouble will either sweeten or embitter us. A classic example of this is seen in Job and his wife. In view of their horrendous sufferings, particularly Job's, she said to him, "Curse God and die!" (Job 2:9). Job's response was, "You speak as one of the foolish women speaks. Shall we indeed accept good from God, and shall we not accept adversity?"

   > Trouble will either sweeten or embitter us.

   How do we react when serious trouble comes? Some helpful New Testament verses to keep in mind when trouble comes are Romans 12:12; 1 Corinthians 10:13; 1 Thessalonians 3:3-4; Hebrews 10:32-34; and James 1:2-3. Ultimately, if not immediately, testing through various trouble is for our good, even though difficult.

2. Living in a sinful world we are bound to encounter inequities in life. Jacob's favoritism of Joseph obviously led to a growing envy and hatred of him by his older brothers. Hatred is a basic characteristic of our sinful nature, the natural man being hostile toward God and abusive, disobedient, and deceptive toward others. The cruel words and actions of Joseph's older brothers reveal the depth of their hatred of him. They cast him into a pit, having stripped him of his tunic of many colors. They mocked him and left him to die. "Man's inhumanity to man" is an expression all too evident today, as well as throughout the history of the world. At least Reuben showed a quality of mercy about him, if not kindness, being responsible for delivering Joseph from death (Gen. 37:20-22).

3. In the providence of God the other brothers tempered their hatred and decided to sell Joseph to a caravan of Ishmaelites headed for Egypt. In view of all this, we need to remember that we neither live nor die to ourselves. Think of the anguish and misery these older brothers brought upon their father. Somewhere along the line, our words and actions will have a reaction and influence on others for good or evil.

4. Among the many helpful lessons of this chapter, none is more significant than the lesson of God's sovereign providence. God's plan will be shown later how each of these events laid the foundation for Him to work and bless.

> Behind our life the Weaver stands
> And works His wondrous will;
> We leave it all in His wise hands,
> And trust His perfect skill.
> Should mystery enshroud His plan,
> And our short sight be dim,
> We will not try the whole to scan,
> But leave each thread to Him.
> –C. Murray

5. As for some practical lessons from this section, we might well ask ourselves: Are we sensitive to the cries and needs of others? Do we think of others only in terms of material values? True contentment is not found in money.

Are we sensitive to the cries and needs of others?

3

TRIAL AND TRIUMPH
(GENESIS 39:1-23)

We will not be commenting on Genesis 38 (especially as, chronologically speaking, the events recorded in it probably occurred prior to the account of Joseph that begins in chapter 37). However, if the student wonders why the sordid details of this chapter are even included in the Genesis record, note at least three reasons: (1) God's Word does not play down sin, even when it is found in the register of the Redeemer's family (38:1-29; Ruth 4:18-22; Matt. 1:3); (2) to contrast Joseph's victory over sin (chapter 39) with Judah's sin and shame; and (3) to display God's matchless and marvelous grace by choosing the tribe of Judah to be the line through which the Redeemer would come, and specifically through a child of his union with Tamar (38:11 and following; Matt. 1:3).

This outstanding chapter (Genesis 39) reveals one of the Bible's great lessons in how to overcome temptation. Temptation lurks all around us, and is a great test of life and character. In Joseph's case, he overcame it; in others this is not always so. Resisting temptation is not easy. Oscar Wilde, the humorist, once attested this when he quipped, "I can resist anything but temptation!"

"This chapter will never fail to appeal to our kind, because that of which it speaks—sexual attraction—lies at the foundation of all social relations. When a young man or woman leaves home—a Christian home—and no longer feels its restraints and constraints, he or she is exposed for the first time to grave dangers. This was Joseph's case, where luxury and laxity reigned, but he believed what it would be well for us to believe—that we can go nowhere beyond the reach of God."

–Scroggie

With these details in mind, let's look now at this chapter, noting Joseph's favor with God and man, Joseph's faithfulness, Joseph's frame-up, and Joseph's fetters.

Joseph's Favor with God and Man (39:1-6)

This paragraph shows what a remarkable young man Joseph was. God's hand of blessing was on him. His favor is observed from a twofold standpoint, the first being his favor *with God* (39:1-2).

Joseph had been sold by the Midianites to Potiphar, "an officer of Pharaoh, captain of the guard" (v. 1). The word "officer" means a eunuch (cf. 2 Kings 20:18; 25:11; Jeremiah 29:2). It was common to require prominent officers in the king's court to be castrated, no doubt to insure complete loyalty to the ruler and to prevent them from yielding to the temptation of establishing a dynasty of their own by a military coup. Since Potiphar was a married man, either he had become a eunuch to acquire high office, or else his wife had married him for social or financial reasons. This might explain why Potiphar's wife may have been prone to sexual weakness and adultery, although she is not to be excused for her behavior.

As the "captain of the guard," which literally means that he was the "chief of the executioners," Potiphar had the power of life and death under the direction of Pharaoh. Thus it was into this kind of situation and society that Joseph was brought, a position that no doubt provided him with certain advantages which were useful to him later on.

Nevertheless, the Lord was with Joseph, and He prospered him resulting in the fact that he gained favor *with man* (39:3-6). Because Potiphar saw that the Lord was with Joseph, he made him overseer of all that he owned. The result? God rewarded Potiphar well for keeping Joseph! The Lord blessed Potiphar's house. The only thing which was a concern to Potiphar was his food, possibly because of Egyptian rules of cleanliness (see 43:32).

> God can and does bring blessing to others through a believer's presence.

There is an interesting lesson in this incident. God blessed the house of Potiphar because of the presence of Joseph. Earlier in Genesis we learn that Laban's household was blessed because of the presence of Jacob,

Joseph's father (30:27). God can and does bring blessing to others through a believer's presence.

Joseph is a good example to all serving believers, high or low (see Colossians 3:23-24; Titus 2:9-10; and 1 Peter 2:18). He was a man of good character, and his success is to be traced to this and to the work that he did. Achievement, not status, is in view here. The world has an eye out for this kind of worker and work. Believers should be faithful employees. Prisoners should be respectful of authority and act in a manner that pleases the Lord.

The last part of verse 6 tells us that Joseph was "handsome in form and appearance." The same thing was said of his mother, Rachel (cf. 29:17). Of only two other men does the Bible say that they were handsome, and they were David and Absalom (1 Sam. 16:12; 2 Sam. 14:25). In a sense, the final words about Joseph in verse 6 prepare us for the attack that his good looks invited.

Joseph's Faithfulness (39:7-12)

By now, Joseph had become an important member of Egyptian society. Since Egypt was in a period of prosperity and ease, it is to be expected that temptation would present itself. Furthermore, the morals of Egyptian women were notoriously bad at this period. The ancients described Egypt as "the home of unchastity," speaking of the great prevalence of marital infidelity.

Potiphar's wife's first approach to Joseph was a sudden, forceful one. It might have seemed wise to yield, but Joseph refused, rightly asking, "How then can I do this great wickedness, and sin against God?" (v. 9). To have sinned in this way would have been to defy God's authority over his life and to abuse His goodness.

This, however, was not the end of things. Joseph was pressured by Potiphar's wife day after day, her design being to coax Joseph into submission. It was here that Samson failed (Judges 14:17; 16:16). Finally, the moment of truth came (vv. 11-12).

There are many examples in the Bible of men and women who remained faithful and responsible during difficult and pressured circumstances. One example is Jeremiah, who was God's major prophet during the decline and fall of the southern kingdom of Judah. He was a courageous man of God who endured persecution and extreme suffering, including prison (Jeremiah 37 and 38). He was called of God to preach a message of judgment to a wayward, sinful people. He prophesied during the reigns of the last five kings of Judah.

A much lesser known prophet, Micaiah, was put in prison by King Ahab of Israel because he did not prophesy what the king wanted to hear (1 Kings 22:7-8, 17-18, 28). Nevertheless, what Micaiah prophesied came true; Ahab died in battle just as he had predicted (1 Kings 22:29-38).

A classic Old Testament example of a faithful woman is found in Esther, the Jewish queen of King Ahasuerus (Xerxes) of Persia. At the risk of her life and under great stress she was used by God to save her people, the Jews, from a plot to destroy them. In the New Testament there are several examples of those who remained faithful regardless of the cost to themselves, even prison (e.g., Peter, James, John, Paul, Aquila and Priscilla, and Andronicus and Junia).

———— ✎ ————
**Was it easy for
Joseph to say no?**
———— ✎ ————

Young people are being told these days to "just say no" to drugs, crime, and premarital sex. That is fine, but it is tough to do so, as any adult who has tried to quit smoking or lose weight knows full well. We also need to keep in mind that the heart of man is capable of rationalizing virtually anything he wants to do (Jer. 17:9). By doing this he seeks to excuse or lessen his guilt and responsibility.

"Do you think it was easy for Joseph to 'just say no' to Mrs. Potiphar? Consider again. (1) He was away from home like a kid off to college or an executive on a business trip. (2) Mrs. Potiphar appealed to a natural desire. (3) Mrs. Potiphar was important. To give her what she wanted could have given Joseph just about anything he wanted. (4) Joseph could have viewed it as a perk he deserved because of his promotions and hard work. (5) She offered repeatedly. How do you 'just say no' when the same alluring forbidden fruit is offered day after day? (6) Nobody else was home—'Nobody will ever know. . . .'

"But Joseph conquered temptation. How? He saw right past Mrs. Potiphar to her husband, who would be hurt deeply if Joseph gave in—Potiphar would lose his best worker and all of the wealth Joseph could bring him. And behind Potiphar, Joseph saw the holy God, who calls sin sin, and to whom sin is deeply, horribly offensive. Through God's eyes, Joseph saw Mrs. Potiphar's proposition for the wicked, repulsive, slimy thing it really was. That's the only way to 'just say no.'"

—Author Unknown

Thus we read in the closing words of verse 12, "he left his garment in her hand, and fled and ran outside."

> Through God's eyes, Joseph saw Mrs. Potiphar's proposition for the wicked, repulsive, slimy thing it really was.

"Joseph heard a voice in his inner man, 'Fly, Joseph, fly; there is no way to escape but by running.' And, leaving his cloak in her hand, the young Hebrew fled. It was one of the most heroic flights in history. Someone has said that opportunity makes a man a criminal, and he had abundant opportunity. Importunity (i.e. entreating, imploring, or pleading) will drive most men astray, and he was subjected to a haunting day-by-day solicitation of the softest and cleverest kind. With a strength more than human he prevailed, taking heed to the Word of God by the grace and power of God. It is better to lose one's coat than one's conscience. Often men say, to excuse their actions, 'We must live,' but, in fact, there are times when we must remember, 'We must die.' To live in the light of the fact that we must face our God is the way to joy and contentment."

—S. Lewis Johnson, Jr.

Joseph's Frame-Up (39:13-18)

It has been said, "Hell hath no fury like a woman scorned." Her pride having been offended, Potiphar's wife lashed out in fury against Joseph and her husband (cf. vv. 14, 17). With the cloak in her hand she posed as the victim! She had won a temporary victory, although there are hints in the text that even her husband did not believe her.

Joseph's Fetters (39:19-23)

No longer was Joseph simply in Egypt; he was in jail. Thus his humiliation was re-enacted at a deeper level. Nevertheless, at the beginning of the chapter and all the way through, the Lord was with Joseph. Even in prison God showed him kindness and favor, the result being that the jailer placed complete trust in him, turning everyone and everything over to his care. Why? Because he recognized the worth of Joseph's character and capabilities. The chapter closes with his integrity crowned by the presence and prosperity of God.

POINTS TO PONDER

1. As for temptation or testing, the Scriptures make it clear that it is a necessary part of human, and especially Christian, experience (see 2 Timothy 3:12 and James 1:12). As for the various sources of temptation, there are at least three: (1) from a physical object that one encounters; (2) from a pressure situation (3) from a voice within saying, "You're worthless. Why try?"

> **Temptation only becomes sin when we yield to it.**

How should we meet temptation? The Bible gives us the key to deal with it from a threefold standpoint: (1) temptation that comes from the urge to conform to the world is met by renewal and transformation (Rom. 12:2); (2) temptation traceable to Satan is met by resistance (James 4:7); and (3) temptation that arises from the lust of the flesh is conquered by flight (1 Cor. 6:18; 2 Tim. 2:22), as Genesis 39 so vividly illustrates.

2. We also learn that it is not a sin to be tempted. Temptation only becomes sin when we yield to it. And Joseph is proof that it is not necessary to sin, but that as individuals we can resist, overcome, and be pure.

> "It has been said that three things kept Joseph pure—duty, honor, and faith. He who has work to do, who is guided by high principle, and who believes in God, is invulnerable to temptation. 'He refused' (v. 8). What hung on that? The future history of Israel. Well, the innocent have often suffered (vv. 20-23). But better to be an innocent slave than a defiled free man."
>
> –Scroggie

But how is victory gained? First, Joseph walked in God's presence, for God was with him. Second, he fought with the weapon of God's Word (see Matthew 4:1-11 and Ephesians 6:17). And third, he learned specific solutions to life's problems. When he was tempted to yield to lust, he fled.

> "The word of God is clear in teaching that there is nothing inherently wrong with sex. God made man with the power for reproduction. But the sin comes when those things which God has so graciously bestowed upon His creatures are used for vile, illicit purposes. Sexual sin was the cardinal offense of the pagan world in Paul's day, and doubtless it still holds first place. Where believers are not yielded to the Holy Spirit, sexual sins often come into their lives and prove their downfall."
>
> –William MacDonald

3. A key means to overcoming sexual temptation is to channel sexual energies and tensions into approved outlets such as sports, a brisk walk, jogging, and social or church activities. The person who seeks to keep busy in the Lord's service has much better control of the urges and tensions of man's lower nature.

4. In addition to prisons of steel, concrete, and razor wire, there are other kinds of "prisons." Multitudes of men and women are bound by prisons of their own making, such as the prison of alcoholism, drug addiction, pornography, and other forms of sexual immorality. In many instances rehabilitation is helpful, but what is really needed is regeneration.

> The person who seeks to keep busy in the Lord's service has much better control of the urges and tensions of man's lower nature.

Such power to stand fast comes only from God. Have you become one of His children through faith in His Son, the Lord Jesus Christ, who suffered, shed His blood, and died for your sins and mine on the cross? That's the first big step. Then we need to want to confess and forsake sin (Prov. 28:13; 1 John 1:9), to constantly yield ourselves to the Lord (Rom. 6:19; 12:1-2), to read, study, meditate on, obey, and memorize God's Word (Ps. 119:9, 11), to spend time day by day in prayer (Matt. 6:13; Col. 4:2), to form close friendships with other Christians (Heb. 10:25), to serve the Lord (1 Cor. 15:58), to discipline the body (1 Cor. 9:27), to control our thought life (Phil. 4:8), and to avoid anything that would lower our resistance to sin, such as alcohol and drugs (Romans 13:14; Jude 23).

4

DIVINE DISCIPLINE IN PHARAOH'S DUNGEON
(GENESIS 40:1-23)

The first two lines of William Cowper's famous hymn are readily illustrated in Genesis 40. They are: "God moves in a mysterious way His wonders to perform."

"The offenses of the cupbearer and the baker were committed by the men in the ordinary course of life, but in the final analysis they were planned by the Lord God with the ultimate welfare of His chosen servant Joseph in mind. It is by them that Joseph comes finally to the attention of the ruler of the land. And it is from that relationship that he is able later to be the deliverer of Jacob and his sons from the famine that devastates the land. And it is in the departure of the chosen family from the land of Egypt that they are preserved from the evils in the land. They are thus kept relatively pure from national pollution, and preserved for the tasks that He had planned for them in the future. As the writer of Proverbs puts it, 'The king's heart is in the hand of the LORD, like the rivers of water; He turns it wherever He wishes' (Proverbs 21:1)."

–Johnson

> Joseph's prison experience was the means of further developing his character.

Through Joseph's encounter with Pharaoh's officers he was better prepared to fit into court life. In addition, through his prison experience Joseph was disciplined for his future task under Pharaoh. Finally, Joseph's prison experience was the means of further developing his character. It was the psalmist who described Joseph's life in prison as follows: "He was laid in irons" (Ps. 105:18), and in a symbolic sense, iron entered into him through this discipline.

The two years that Joseph spent in prison meant the same to him as the time in the desert did to Moses, exile did to Daniel, and the years in Arabia did to the apostle Paul.

Pharaoh's Imprisonment of His Court Officers (40:1-4)

"The chief cupbearer and the chief baker" (v. 2, NASB)—these being their correct designations—had suddenly been put in prison by Pharaoh. Why, we don't know. The chief cupbearer was responsible for handling Pharaoh's wines; the chief baker was responsible for Pharaoh's bread and other delicacies. Neither man had an easy task.

> "Had there been an attempt at poisoning in the palace? Suspicion would fall on the butler or the baker; so, in the absence of evidence, both were put into prison; and what the wisest in Egypt could not divine, this Spirit-moved Hebrew slave disclosed—namely, that it was the baker who was guilty."
>
> –Scroggie

The prison house, where Joseph was being kept, was evidently attached to Potiphar's house. The two officers were put in this jail and Joseph was assigned to serve them, this being a further token of Potiphar's trust of Joseph. It was not a comfortable or pleasant place. In fact, Joseph described it in verse 15 as "the dungeon." The word he used literally means a hole.

Joseph Interprets Two Dreams (40:5-19)

Dreams played an important part in ancient times, and we see evidence of that in this portion of Genesis. There are two in Genesis 37, two here, and two in the next chapter. Also, there are different kinds of dreams: divine dreams (28:12; 41:17; Dan. 2:28), diabolical dreams (Deut. 13:1-2; Jer. 23:16; 27:9), and natural dreams (Eccl. 5:3). It is interesting to note that in the Bible only two Israelites engaged in the interpretation of dreams, Joseph and Daniel, and each of them were connected with a pagan ruler, the one in Egypt and the other in Mesopotamia, the very lands in which oneiromancy (the foretelling of events by dreams) developed.

Is it possible that God could speak to someone in a dream today? Yes, since "with God all things are possible" (Matt. 19:26). Dreams, however, are unreliable and we could easily be led astray by them. Today we have God's complete written revelation in the Scriptures. To discern His will and hear His voice we need to daily search the written Word of God in dependence on the Holy Spirit to reveal His perfect will to our hearts and minds.

> ❧
>
> **Today we have God's complete written revelation in the Scriptures.**
>
> ❧

While in prison the chief cupbearer and the chief baker had dreams, but they were depressed because they were unable to interpret them. Upon observing their dejection and learning the reason for it, Joseph said, "Do not interpretations belong to God? Tell them to me, please" (v. 8). Evidently, Joseph was conscious of being a prophet of God, at the same time revealing his intimacy with Him and loyalty to Him.

Barnhouse tells the story of a little boy who told a friend, "My father and I know everything." When the other boy asked a very hard question at this point, the first one replied, "That's one for my father." Joseph had this same kind of simple and complete confidence in God. God can solve all problems, including whatever problem you or I may have at this present time.

The chief cupbearer dreamed that he saw a vine. It had three branches which budded and blossomed, and its cluster brought forth grapes. In his dream Pharaoh's cup was in his hand. He squeezed the grapes into the king's cup and gave it to him (vv. 9-11).

Joseph gave the chief cupbearer a favorable interpretation of his dream: in three days, he would be restored to his position in Pharaoh's court. It was then that Joseph said, "But remember me when it is well with you, and please show kindness to me; make mention of me to Pharaoh, and get me out of this house. For indeed I was stolen away from the land of the Hebrews; and also I have done nothing here that they should put me into the dungeon" (vv. 14-15). Was Joseph right in requesting of the cupbearer what he did? Some say yes, and some say no. Whatever one may think, it was only natural for Joseph to ask what he did, and I do not think he is to be criticized for a lack of faith in doing so. After all, we were not there, and we should resist the temptation to be "armchair specialists."

One thing is certain—heavenly joy and satisfaction do not come to us by our own efforts but by letting God work out all the details according to His will and timetable.

Thinking that his dream might have a favorable interpretation also, the baker told his to Joseph (vv. 16-17). It too related to his occupation, casting some light on the professional standards of his work. However, the interpretation was not a good one (vv. 18-19). The baker would be hung on a tree so that the birds of prey might eat his flesh.

Joseph here revealed his courage in making known the foreboding interpretation of the baker's dream. There is a lesson here for us. We must not tailor our message to suit our hearers. We must give it whether it is pleasant or unpleasant.

The Dreams Are Fulfilled (40:20-23)

Just as Joseph had interpreted his dream, three days later on Pharaoh's birthday, the cupbearer was restored to his office and work. And in accordance with Joseph's interpretation of his dream, the baker's head was "lifted up" as he was hung.

One of the characteristics of humanity in general is a lack of gratitude, and sadly this is illustrated here. It could be, however, that the cupbearer's forgetfulness was intentional, not wanting to remind Pharaoh that he had at one time been out of his good graces.

POINTS TO PONDER

1. We quote two more lines from William Cowper's hymn: "Behind a frowning Providence there is a smiling face." Sold into slavery, falsely accused, imprisoned, forgotten—all these things seem like God was frowning on Joseph. However, behind the scenes God was working all these details together for His glory and for Joseph's blessing.

2. We see how seemingly insignificant circumstances, such as the two men Joseph served, have their meaning in life, even in prison.

3. Although his circumstances were difficult, we observe that Joseph remained faithful to God and to his convictions. Yet we are given a little glimpse of his humanity in verses 14 and 15. He found prison hard and longed for freedom, but while there he performed his duties faithfully and interested himself in others.

> **Although his circumstances were difficult, Joseph remained faithful to God and to his convictions.**

4. We observe from Joseph's experience in prison that patient waiting on God is extremely important in all of life's circumstances. Even though totally innocent of the charges against him, Joseph waited two years for God to act on his behalf. This experience matured his character for his life-work which lay ahead of him.

5. We see from this account how God's timing is crucial. God is never ahead of His time, and He is never behind either.

6. We note that the heart in touch with God will always find His grace sufficient no matter how difficult the circumstances.

> **Patient waiting on God is extremely important in all of life's circumstances.**

"In spite of everything that was against him, Joseph was victorious by the grace of God. Whether it was silence after calumny (i.e., false accusation of a crime or misconduct) and injustice, whether it was cheerfulness amidst hardship, whether it was quick sympathy with the sorrows of others, whether it was patient endurance amidst hopes deferred, he was more than conqueror; and the secret of it all was, 'the Lord was with him.'

"The test of character lies in the spirit of being unprovoked, though faced by constant friction and opposition; and the test of ideal service is its continuance when unrecognized. True life consists in going on, without placing any limit to goodness of character or faithfulness of service, even though neither should be acknowledged on earth; and this is only possible by the grace of God."

–Thomas

To illustrate all of this, Griffith Thomas tells about a certain coal mining area, where almost everything was covered with coal dust except a beautiful white flower. When someone who was strange to the place remarked that the owner must take very great care of the flower to prevent it from being covered with coal dust, another who was standing by threw on the flower some dust which immediately fell off, leaving its whiteness and beauty as exquisite as ever. The explanation was that the flower had on it what might be called an enamel which enabled it to receive the dust and throw it off without feeling anything of its effects. So it was with Joseph. His character was covered with the enamel of divine grace, and all these sorrows and troubles which came upon him left him untouched except for the increased strength and power bestowed on him by God.

5

FROM PRISON TO PRIME MINISTER
(GENESIS 41:1-57)

A simple way to handle a long chapter like this one is to center its primary subject matter around key words. This is precisely what W. Graham Scroggie did in his study of it, and I readily acknowledge my indebtedness to him for all but the second and last key words used to emphasize the significant points of the narrative. The words are: *Revelation* (vv. 1-8); *Association* (vv. 9-13); *Interpretation* (vv. 14-32); *Recommendation* (vv. 33-36); *Exaltation* (vv. 37-45); and *Administration* (vv. 46-57).

Among other things, this chapter again places stress on at least three familiar truths. The first is the doctrine of the providence of God. He is working all things together for good (Rom. 8:28), or as the New International Version translates this classic text: "And we

> — ❧ —
> **God is working all things together for good.**
> — ❧ —

know that *in* all things God works for the good of those who love Him, who have been called according to His purpose" (emphasis added). The second great truth is the necessity to place one's faith in God and not in man (Isa. 2:22).

> "We need human sympathy, companionship, and love, and we enjoy the encouragement of our fellowmen. Men, however, always fail us, and even the best disappoint us. On the other hand, the Lord abides faithful. He cannot promise and then fail to fulfill His word. He may make us wait, and He may delay the coming of the relief. . . . He may allow your prayers to accumulate like unopened letters on the table of an absent friend. But at last He will say, 'O man, O woman, great is thy faith: be it unto thee even as thou wilt.'

Therefore, let us avoid the feverishness of impatience, and let us wait in confidence on the Lord. 'Rest in the LORD, and wait patiently for Him' (Ps. 37:7). 'Wait on the LORD, and keep His way, and He shall exalt you to inherit the land; when the wicked are cut off, you shall see it' (v. 34)."

–Johnson

The final great truth stressed in this chapter centers on the Lord Jesus Christ. The exaltation of Joseph to Pharaoh's right hand, after the humiliation and suffering of his previous years of faithful service, clearly pictures Christ in His passage from humiliation through death to exaltation to the right hand of the throne of God.

With these things in mind, let's focus on our first key word.

Revelation (41:1-8)

After two full years (which must have seemed like the longest two years in Joseph's life), Pharaoh had a dream. Essentially, the dream was for Joseph's benefit, not Pharaoh's, but it was the king who had the dream.

We are again reminded of King Solomon's words: "The king's heart is in the hand of the LORD, like the rivers of water; He turns it wherever He wishes" (Prov. 21:1). Having dreamed that he was by the Nile River, Pharaoh saw seven ugly and gaunt cows eating up seven sleek and fat ones. This is a typical Egyptian picture, since cows often stand almost submerged in the river for refuge from heat and flies. Egyptians and Babylonians specialized in the interpretation of dreams and, as a result, took a keen interest in them. This was a method God used in those days to instruct unbelieving hearts.

Again, Pharaoh's second dream (vv. 5-7) was a typical Egyptian one, since Egypt was the granary of the ancient world. In this dream seven thin ears of grain swallowed up seven plump and good ones. The uniqueness of these dreams startled and troubled the king. Somehow, all the magicians and wise men of Egypt could not interpret the rather obvious dreams (v. 8), indicating that it was God who blinded their minds to their meaning (see Daniel 2:2).

The magicians of Joseph's day remind us of those who appeared later in Moses' time (Ex. 7-9; see 2 Timothy 3:8). They worked signs and wonders beyond the ordinary powers of man and were undoubtedly energized by Satan. The wise men are closely identified in Scripture with magicians and are referred to as astrologers (Dan. 1:20; 2:2; Matt. 2:1, 7, 16; Acts 13:6, 8).

> "As it is well known, Egypt stands in Scripture as a figure of the world. In Joseph's time, the land of the Pharaoh's was the center of learning and culture, the proud leader of the ancient civilizations. But the people were idolaters. They knew not God, and only in His light can we see light. Apart from Him, all is darkness, morally and spiritually. So we see it in the chapter before us. The magicians were impotent, the wise men displayed their ignorance, and Pharaoh was made to feel the powerlessness of all human resources and the worthlessness of all human wisdom."
>
> –Arthur W. Pink

Association (41:9-13)

Thanks to the chief cupbearer's association of dreams with Joseph, the wheels were set in motion for Joseph's release. Evidently the cupbearer was present at this meeting of the minds.

> "A sluggish memory may easily cause another much pain. Is there anyone whom you have wrongly forgotten? Remember your fault this day (v. 9). Joseph had dreamed of sheaves and stars; Pharaoh dreams of cows and corn. Why, in each case, is the dream doubled (v. 32)? Compare our Lord's double parables. Repetition in Scripture is for the purpose of emphasis; to denote certainty, and, frequently, to present two aspects of one thing. That the same thing was pointed by each of Pharaoh's dreams was obvious; but its identity was not obvious. So in come the magicians and philosophers—men with empty heads behind high brows, so far as dreams were concerned, anyway (v. 8). But the failure of these pundits was good for one prisoner; their prophetic bankruptcy led to the termination of his physical bondage. Joseph was now thirty years of age (v. 46); he had been away from home for about twelve years, which was the period of his special preparation for the great task which lay before him. Be patient."
>
> –Scroggie

Interpretation (41:14-32)

Quickly, the king had Joseph brought from prison, but first Joseph had to shave his head—his Egyptian sign of mourning—and change his clothes (v. 14).

> "Never, surely, was there so rapid a transformation! How a man behaves himself in such circumstances is revealing. Remember, Joseph was only thirty, but he no more lost his head when brought into the palace than he lost his faith when thrown into the prison. He kept an even keel in all waters."
>
> –Scroggie

Pharaoh's flattering words did not unnerve Joseph; the latter simply pointed out that God alone interprets dreams (v. 15). Having promised Pharaoh an answer that would promote the king's well-being, Joseph refused to take advantage of the situation. To Joseph, the guarding of God's honor was more important (see Psalm 16:8).

> In the palace Joseph would not take credit for good which belonged to God.

> "As in Potiphar's house he would not compromise with evil which belonged to the Devil, so in the prison and in the palace he would not take credit for good which belonged to God."
>
> –Scroggie

Having repeated his dreams to Joseph, with the additional details of verses 19 and 21, Joseph gave Pharaoh a clear interpretation. In verse 28, Joseph repeated what he had said in verse 25—namely, that God had shown Pharaoh what He was about to do. These verses, along with the emphasis in verse 32, represent a call for action in view of the imminent certainty of the fulfillment of Pharaoh's dreams.

Recommendation (41:33-36)

At this point, Joseph gave more than an interpretation. He provided Pharaoh with a complete economic program to meet the unusual emergency that faced the nation. It involved a discerning and wise chief administrator, assistant administrators, a double tithe by way of tax during the years of plenty, and a plan for the storage of the excess grain in the cities (the logical place) as a reserve for the future years of famine. We can be sure that

Joseph was not thinking of anything more than his own possible release from prison.

Exaltation (41:37-45)

The plan appealed to Pharaoh and all his servants. Just what Pharaoh understood by the term "divine spirit" in verse 38 is difficult to determine, but it at least suggested the supernatural. If it is a reference to the Holy Spirit, then it is the Bible's first mention of the Holy Spirit coming on a man and empowering him (for another example, see Exodus 28:3). At any rate, Joseph was chosen by Pharaoh to be Egypt's Prime Minister. He certified it by giving Joseph the ring from his hand, clothing him in fine linen and a gold chain, and having him ride in the king's second chariot. These things spoke respectively of the king's authority, court dress, approval, and exaltation to the supreme authority under the king.

In addition, Pharaoh named Joseph "Zaphenath-paneah," a name honoring Joseph's God and meaning "revealer of secret things." Joseph was also given an Egyptian wife named Asenath. He then made an inspection tour of the entire land (v. 45).

Administration (41:46-57)

Joseph's age is given here: thirty. It is remarkable that a man this young should have such a position. As someone has said,

> Only a man like Joseph, schooled by adversity and sorrow, could meet a sudden elevation like this without pride and self-exaltation.

"Only a man like Joseph, schooled by adversity and sorrow, could meet a sudden elevation like this without pride and self-exaltation. His rigorous training enabled him to encounter success without succumbing to its blandishments."

Two sons were born to Joseph and his wife (vv. 50-52). Manasseh means "forgetting," while Ephraim means "fruitful," the two meanings being something of a summary of his life to that point. It should not be read into the meaning of Manasseh's name that Joseph no longer cared about his father's household. Rather, it means that the sting of his past experiences had left him. God had brought him into a place of fruitfulness, as emphasized in the meaning of Ephraim's name.

The seven years of famine happened according to Joseph's interpretation of Pharaoh's dreams, just as the years of plenty did. Through his wise management, a catastrophe was averted—not only in Egypt, but in all the countries near and far.

F. B. Meyer (1847-1929) beautifully summarized as follows the sovereign providence and purposes of God as fulfilled through Joseph:

"It was a wonderful ascent, sheer in a single bound from the dungeon to the steps of the throne. His father had rebuked him [see Genesis 37:10], now Pharaoh, the greatest monarch of his time, welcomes him. His brethren despised him; now the proudest priesthood of the world opens its ranks to receive him by marriage into their midst, considering it wiser to conciliate a man who was from that moment to be the greatest force in Egyptian politics and life. The hands that were hard with the toils of a slave are adorned with a signet ring. The feet are no longer tormented by fetters; a chain of gold is linked around his neck. The coat of many colors torn from him by violence and defiled by blood, and the garment left in the hands of the adulteress, are exchanged for vestures of fine linen drawn from the royal wardrobe. He was once trampled upon as the off scouring of all things; now all Egypt is commanded to bow down before him, as he rides forth in the second chariot, prime minister of Egypt, and second only to the king."

POINTS TO PONDER

1. God has a useful purpose for each one of His children (Eph. 2:10)

2. God is working all things together for His glory and for our good (Rom. 8:28).

3. Unlikely circumstances are sometimes used by God to prepare us for His purpose and place (e.g., Joseph in prison; Moses in the desert for 40 years; Paul in Arabia).

4. God is faithful; He will not fail us (1 Cor. 10:13). Our part is to trust Him, even when he seems far away and indifferent to our circumstances (Prov. 3:5-6).

5. God asks us to be faithful whether we are in need or prospering (Phil. 4:12).

6. Others should see something of God's presence in us evidenced by our righteous living (1 Peter 2:12).

7. We should give God the credit for any good that comes to us, not seeking in any way to take the glory that belongs to Him alone.

8. God will always honor His children who are faithful to Him, for He has said, "Those who honor me I will honor" (1 Sam. 2:30).

As we meditate on the details of Joseph's life, we cannot help but think of Joseph's Lord and His future kingdom over all the earth, all made possible by virtue of His sufferings and atoning death followed by His exaltation to God's right hand.

Have you yielded to the Savior, the Lord Jesus Christ, the King of kings and Lord of lords?

———— ✢ ————

Unlikely circumstances are sometimes used by God to prepare us for His purpose and place.

———— ✢ ————

6

THE GOADING OF A GUILTY CONSCIENCE
(GENESIS 42:1-38)

Genesis 42 is an especially important chapter because it records the first visit of Joseph's brothers to Egypt.

"More than twenty years have passed since Joseph was sold by his brethren. We know what he had been doing; but what had they been doing? *Trying to forget!* Joseph had been doing that too, and so he called his first son *Manasseh* (41:51); but he had been forgetting the injury done to him, whereas they had been forgetting the injury they had done."

–Scroggie

> **"Whatever a man sows, that he will also reap."**

Through a series of ordinary events, Joseph's brothers were made to recall with great intensity their sinful act more than twenty years before. Verses 21 and 22 record their own confession of guilt.

There's an old English proverb which says, "A guilty conscience needs no accuser." Standing before an apparently harsh governor of Egypt and faced with the necessity of bringing Benjamin with them on their next trip to Egypt, the brothers' consciences were pricked, and we have a classic illustration of the age-old principle, "Whatever a man sows, that he will also reap" (Gal. 6:7).

As Scroggie has further commented,

> "A crime is no less a crime at the end of twenty years than when it was committed; and all sin must be judged sooner or later. Joseph has been blamed for not revealing himself to his brethren at once, but that is a shallow view, and quite misses the moral necessity for Joseph's course of action. A sinner must have his guilt brought home to him. There can be no repentance without that, and where there is no repentance there cannot be forgiveness. Moral processes work more slowly than mechanical processes, and love can be patient."

The Command of Jacob (42:1-2)

Evidently the famine was becoming severe in Canaan, but Jacob had heard that there was grain in Egypt. He was still head of the household, so he ordered his sons, who apparently were taking no initiative to solve the problem, to go to Egypt to buy grain.

The Contact of the Brothers with Joseph (42:3-17)

The brothers made their way to Egypt to buy grain without Benjamin, Joseph's younger brother and other son of Rachel. Why did Benjamin remain home? Perhaps because of a certain carefulness in view of the loss of Joseph. Or it may have been that Jacob did not quite trust the other brothers. They had covered up their crimes, but under their father's watchful eye they could not cover up their character.

According to God's providence it was the need of food that marked the first step that led to the brothers' conviction of their sin.

> "But when the mighty famine came, the hearts of these men were opened to conviction; their carnal security was shattered; and they were prepared for certain spiritual experiences of which they would never have dreamed . . . It is so that God deals with us. He breaks up our nest. He sends a mighty famine which cuts away the whole staff of bread. And at such times, weary, worn, and sad, we are prepared to confess our sins, and to receive the words of Christ, when He says, 'Come unto Me, all ye that labor and are heavy laden, and I will give you rest.'"

> –Meyer

The word for "governor" (v. 6) is a very strong Hebrew word which is also translated "ruler." There is a partial fulfillment of Joseph's early dreams in the coming of Joseph's brothers and their bowing down before him (37:7). They, of course, did not realize this, and of course Benjamin was not present (there were eleven sheaves in Joseph's dream; see 37:9).

Again, providentially, Joseph was on hand when his brothers came to buy food. He recognized *them,* but they did not recognize *him.* Remember that Joseph was clean-shaven like the Egyptians, and his brothers would have been bearded. Joseph's dress and bearing as governor made it difficult for them to see and know him in that kind of circumstance. Also, about twenty-two years had passed since they had last seen him.

Joseph's rough treatment of his brothers was not vindictive (see vv. 16-19, 24; 44:9-10). Rather, it was a test to see if there was any change in their attitudes and if there was any conviction of sin and guilt over their treatment of him.

The words of verse 9 indicate that Joseph may have recognized God's providence in their presence before him. However, Benjamin was missing and he would become the focal point of further testing the character of his brothers. Martin Luther was correct in pointing out that Joseph's dealings with his brothers are like those that God uses in dealing with sinners who are being led to repentance.

> Joseph's dealings with his brothers are like those that God uses in dealing with sinners who are being led to repentance.

The defense of his brothers was an honest one (vv. 10-13). That they were "all one man's sons" (v. 11) truthfully indicates to a "stranger" that they may not all have had the same mother. They affirmed that the youngest was with their father, although they were vague about Joseph (v. 13). At this point, however, nothing is revealed about their true attitude of heart. Thus Joseph repeated his charge that they were spies (v. 14 with v. 9) and made an almost unreasonable demand that they all stay in Egypt, while one would return to Canaan to bring back Benjamin. That would test the truthfulness of their claims.

At this point, Joseph put his brothers in prison for three days, a reminder of their treatment of him many years before.

The Condition Presented by Joseph (42:18-20)

Believing that three days were enough to prick their conscience, Joseph now made a modified proposition. One of them would stay, while the rest would return home, taking food, and then they would return to Egypt with their youngest brother. Thus the life of the one remaining would hang in the balance.

It is noteworthy that in verse 18 Joseph gave his brothers one clue, but they did not respond: he said, "I fear God." As Scroggie has commented. "If they had thought more of God than themselves, they might well have wondered how an Egyptian Prime Minister, as they thought him to be, knew God."

The Contrition of the Brothers (42:21-24)

It is here that their guilt over Joseph surfaced. Their consciences were awakened. It was A. T. Pierson who pointed out to W. H. Griffith Thomas that all the elements of repentance are here:

> All the elements of repentance are here: conscience, memory, and reason.

1. Conscience—"We are truly guilty"
2. Memory—"We saw the anguish"
3. Reason—"Therefore this distress has come upon us."

Reuben was more merciful than the others when they originally betrayed him (37:21-22), but here he makes himself out to be better than he really was (37:29-30).

At this point (vv. 23-24), Joseph was overcome with emotion, yet he showed great restraint as well. Having gained his composure, he detained Simeon—perhaps because he was next oldest to Reuben, or maybe because Joseph thought he needed the confinement more than the others since he was the cruelest of the brothers (see 34:25; 49:5-7).

The Concern of the Brothers (42:25-28)

The governor did for his family what he wanted to do: he gave them food without charge. However, the discovery of the money struck terror in the brothers' hearts, since it left them open to the charge of theft. Notice now the keenness of their consciences. They were so overwhelmed that they said, "What is this that God has done to us?"

The Climax of the Brothers' Return Home (42:29-38)

Their report is just a simple restatement of the events recorded in the preceding verses. An even greater fear than before overtook the brothers, and now Jacob himself. All of the men were open to a serious charge.

Their father's charge in this verse strikes very close to the truth: "You have bereaved me of my children." Here, Jacob lapsed in his faith and courage, anticipating the loss of three more of his sons, and seeing all these circumstances against him. Actually, things were progressing toward the climax of getting Joseph back!

Reuben's extravagant and unreasonable offer (vv. 37-38) makes no difference to Jacob. His mind was made up; Benjamin would not go with them to Egypt. By his reference to "Sheol," Jacob simply referred to the place of the departed dead.

POINTS TO PONDER

1. The persistence of God's purpose is readily seen. Men and women often fail to carry through their purposes, but not God. He carries out whatever His will decrees, even though at times He may act ever so slowly from our standpoint.

2. We note the goading power of a guilty conscience. Time does not heal the guilt of sin, although an unrepentant person may develop a seared (hardened) conscience. The best thing to do is to confess our sin and receive God's forgiveness.

    > True repentance requires that we are sufficiently sorry to give up our sin.

3. We observe the elements of true repentance. It is not enough to simply be sorry for our sin—often we are only sorry that we were caught! True repentance requires that we are sufficiently sorry to give up our sin. I recall someone once saying, "You have to be sorry enough to quit!" It was John the Baptist who forcefully proclaimed to the Pharisees and Sadducees, "Brood of vipers! Who has warned

you to flee from the wrath to come? Therefore bear fruits worthy of repentance" (Matt. 3:7-8).

4. We have a classic illustration of the blindness and irrationality of human reasoning in Jacob's conclusion of verse 36. In reality, things were working together for his good. Do we really believe "that all things work together for good to those who love God, to those who are the called according to His purpose" (Rom. 8:28)?

CHAPTER

7

FRUSTRATION, FEAR, AND FAVOR
(GENESIS 43:1-34)

In commenting on this chapter, S. Lewis Johnson, Jr. wrote:

"Behind the scenes that move before the reader of this chapter is the continuing lesson of the mingling together of the purposes of God and His providential government of all things. Far in the background of the several chapters of this section of Genesis is the plan of God to remove the people of God, represented by Jacob and his family, down into the land of Egypt. They need preservation from the corrupting evil of the inhabitants of the land, the Canaanites. And they must live in Egypt as a unified nation.

"There is a problem, however. The brothers have sold one of their own into slavery in Egypt, so they have thought. Thus, they are guilty of a grievous sin against him, and God cannot overlook that sin. It has separated them from the Lord, and it has separated them from the spirit of their father Jacob. It must be dealt with, and that involves conviction, repentance, and reconciliation. The movement of events in the life of Joseph, now the Prime Minister of Egypt, is directed toward those goals."

The Frustration of Jacob (43:1-14)

We don't know just how long it took for the grain to be used up which Jacob's sons had brought from Egypt. It may have been only a few months. However, the famine in Canaan was still "severe," although not total (see v. 11), and another trip to Egypt was necessary.

With the grain having been consumed, it is Jacob himself who again takes the lead in proposing a second journey to the land of the Nile. Thus he instructed his sons, "Go back, buy us a little food."

Had it not been for the famine, Jacob would never have considered going to Egypt for food. Furthermore, he was stubbornly opposed to the idea of sending Benjamin to Egypt. He feared losing him and also seemed not to fully trust his sons. Upon commanding them to go again to Egypt, it is Judah who acts as the spokesman, reminding his father that the governor had solemnly warned them that they would not even see his face if they did not bring Benjamin with them. Judah's ultimatum is given in verses 4 and 5.

Judah had a bad record (see Genesis 38), but a change in his character is observed, and from this point on we see him as a man of intellectual and moral strength. Remember, Jacob had made a vow that Benjamin must stay home (42:38), but Judah knew that the tenor of the governor's demand was not to be trifled with. This was a source of further frustration for Jacob, yet Judah was actually helping his father to make an inevitable decision. Jacob's negative attitude is true to life (v. 6; 42:36), and we see the "old" Jacob (his fleshly, independent nature) at this point. In holding on to his advantage over those who had wronged him, he was actually jeopardizing himself and his sons, including Benjamin.

Again, focusing on Judah,

> "His first word is an ultimatum. In Judah's second speech we should mark his sense of urgency (v. 8), his pledge of honor (v. 9), and his daring confidence (v. 10). Observe that in this narrative the father is called Israel, not Jacob, who speaks in verse 12. Judah had revived his spirit, and he braces himself for the next event."
>
> –Scroggie

> **Although weak and human in so many ways, Jacob possessed a basic trust in God.**

Resigned to what must be done, Jacob gives in. He then characteristically instructs his sons to take a gift to Egypt's governor, as well as money to buy grain and also the money which was given back to them on their first visit (vv. 11-14). His final words to them in verse 14 are a prayer. Although weak and human in so many ways, Jacob possessed a basic trust in God. He sought to exhaust all human expedients, but finally the old patriarch commits them all, and especially Benjamin, to the care of "God Almighty." The term he uses is *El Shaddai*, the omnipotent God, his words being a powerful blessing prayed in faith. Slowly but surely, the old Jacob is beginning to live up to his God-given name, Israel.

The Fear of Joseph's Brothers (43:15-30)

Scroggie rather humorously wrote,

> "These men are getting to know the road which lies between Hebron and Memphis: this is the third time they are treading it! The first time all was new and strange, and they wondered what the land was like to which they were going, and how they would fare. The second time their guilt had awakened. Simeon was left behind, and they had Jacob to face about Benjamin. The third time Benjamin is with them, and they dread the second meeting with 'the lord of the land.' The difference is not in the road, but in the travelers. It is always so!"

Having made their way to Egypt, they eventually found themselves in the presence of Joseph, who in turn instructed his house steward to take them to his home. In all that Joseph put his brothers through, he was not merely trifling with human feelings. Rather, it seems that he was divinely guided in the thorough discipline of his wayward brothers.

Fear gripped the men when they learned they were going to Joseph's house, believing that it was because of the problem of the money found in their sacks (v. 18), so they immediately started to explain everything to the house steward (vv. 19-22).

The steward's response indicates that Joseph had taught him to fear the God of the Hebrews (v. 23). Further, he knew all about the money, even suggesting that it had been supernaturally supplied. To further assure them that everything was all right, Simeon was released from prison and restored to them.

> "The fear of the brethren is in the line of the fear that characterizes all men who stand in rebellion against the Lord God. It is seen first in the fear of Adam and Eve at the presence of the Lord God in the Garden of Eden, for they hid themselves from His presence when He came to them in the cool of the day for fellowship. It has

characterized all men since then (cf. Heb. 2:14-15). It is the product of the sense of unforgiven sin, or guilt. When the gospel invitation is proclaimed, it is natural to human nature unredeemed to be fearful, to be suspicious of God, to be engaged in the fortifying of their position by lame excuses, to strive against submission in faith, rather than to yield gladly to the gracious invitation of a God who has Himself paid the penalty for the sin of sinners and now invites all to enter into permanent union and communion with Him. Oh! the foolishness of the fear of God's gracious appeals to men!"

–S. Lewis Johnson, Jr.

The present that Jacob had told them to bring was given to Joseph, accompanied by their bowing down to him (v. 26). After Joseph asked and learned about their father, they again paid homage (v. 28), their actions unconsciously fulfilling 37:7-11.

Observe the touching scene here. Benjamin was Joseph's full brother, both having been the sons of Rachel. At this point, Joseph was so emotionally overcome he had to leave the room and then broke down and wept (see 42:24). The word translated "deeply stirred" (v. 30, NASB) is a forceful one and means "to grow warm and tender" (see Lamentations 1:20; see also Hosea 11:8, where it refers to Jehovah's warm and tender love for the nation Israel; and 1 Kings 3:26, where it refers to a mother's love for a child).

> Oh! the foolishness of the fear of God's gracious appeals to men!

The Favor of Benjamin (43:31-34)

What a truly great man Joseph was! He had not been spoiled by his exalted position or by the luxury of the palace. Having gained control of himself, he instructed his servants to set his brothers apart from himself and from the Egyptians according to the ritual of the land. (Egyptians looked upon foreigners as unclean, much as Jews later viewed Gentiles.)

To their astonishment, Joseph seated them according to their age (v. 33). We can only wonder what their thoughts were at this point. In observing that a greater portion of food was given to Benjamin they had an opportunity to show jealousy, but they passed the test with flying colors. Joseph's action was an expression of his strong fraternal love for Benjamin.

POINTS TO PONDER

1. Our faith sometimes falters and we tend to look on the dark side of things. However, if we are willing to continue to face the facts as Jacob did, faith, strength, and courage are restored. As a result, we gain the victory over our circumstances with the consciousness that all is part of God's will.

2. God often uses the moral power of the fear of judgment to prove, search, guide, warn, and purify us (see Genesis 42:28; 43:18). Fear helps us shrink from sin, as well as keeping the heart sensitive to God's will. Indeed, as the Scripture affirms, "The fear of the LORD is the beginning of wisdom" (Prov. 9: 10).

3. Many of the tests to which God subjects us are found in the little, ordinary, hidden things of life. It is in these that we reveal what we really are. The prolonged and severe discipline to which Joseph's brothers were subjected was necessary for their moral and spiritual training. They had an important place in God's future plan for Israel. Therefore, a deep work of spiritual correction and preparation had to be implemented.

> **Many of the tests to which God subjects us are found in the little, ordinary, hidden things of life.**

4. It is easy for us to misinterpret God's dealings with us (e.g., Jacob's reaction to his circumstances in Genesis 42:36). As believers we sometimes mistake God's discipline for punishment, failing to realize that "whom the LORD loves He chastens, and scourges every son whom He receives" (Heb. 12:6).

5. Spiritual blessing will never be realized apart from genuine repentance and faith in the Lord Jesus Christ. Simply being conscious of sin is not enough. There must be the evidence of true repentance and faith. Griffith Thomas has said, "Consciousness of sin must always issue in conversion from sin. God cannot act without our repentance. There will always be a barrier to His blessing unless we are prepared to turn from sin with a hearty and true repentance."

6. Joseph's tears were not a sign of weakness. On the contrary, beneath his outer austerity they revealed his heart of tender love for his brother Benjamin. His love for his brother is a picture of the Lord's love for His people. It is not a shame for a man to weep. Remember, "Jesus wept" (John 11:35). It would be well if we shed more tears on behalf of others than we do, particularly on behalf of wayward brothers and sisters (see 1 Peter 4:8 with Galatians 6:1). God grant that we might shed more tears of love!

CHAPTER

8

JOSEPH AND JUDAH
(GENESIS 44:1-34)

This chapter records the final steps in the ongoing story of God's discipline of Jacob and his sons. It is a testimony to divine perseverance; God never lets up until His work is finished. Furthermore, the chapter presses home the point that He knows all about our iniquity, since nothing is hidden from His sight. "All things are naked and open to the eyes of Him to whom we must give account" (Heb. 4:13).

———— ❧ ————
God never lets up until His work is finished.
———— ❧ ————

The story is told of a man who was able to join the Emperor of China's orchestra, although he could not play a note. Whenever the orchestra played, he would hold his flute against his lips, not daring even to blow softly for fear he might cause a discord. He received a modest salary and was able to live comfortably.

One day, the emperor happened to desire that each musician play a solo for him. The flutist became desperate. He tried to take quick professional lessons, but to no avail, for he really had no ear for music. He pretended to be sick, but the royal physician who attended him knew better, causing him to be all the more anxious. Tragically, on the day of his solo appearance he took poison rather than attempt to play any music. And as you might guess, there comes from this incident not only the familiar Chinese proverb, "He dared not face the music," but our own familiar expression about "facing the music."

For quite a while now, Joseph's brothers had been led along step by step to a point of "facing the music" in relation to their sin. It is in these verses that they are led to that climactic point, just prior to Joseph's revelation of himself to them. God's desire was to bring Joseph's brothers to true repentance, so He relentlessly pursued them until they came to terms with their sin.

Joseph's Masterful Plan (44:1-17)

Joseph's instruction to the house steward to have his silver cup placed in Benjamin's sack to create the impression that he had stolen it was indeed clever. The issue was, would the brothers abandon Benjamin to his fate as they had abandoned Joseph years before? When Joseph's steward caught up with them, he said that the one in whose sack the cup was found would have to be left in Egypt as a slave (v. 10). The stakes were high. The brothers were even harsher, for they said that the guilty party should die, and that the rest should become slaves (v. 9).

> "This is a strange story, but we must understand that Joseph was not playing with his brethren; however strange the procedure was we may be sure a moral purpose lay behind it. What then was that purpose? It was to discover whether or not the ten were the selfish, treacherous, and cruel men now that they had been twenty years before; it was to see whether, in a crisis like this, they would abandon their youngest brother to save themselves. . . . We can imagine what a happy company it was now passing over the road for the fourth time; going back to Jacob with food, and Simeon, and Benjamin. Suddenly their joy is stayed, their song ceases, and they are charged with theft. What an hour was that when the sacks were being searched, and what a moment when the cup was found in Benjamin's! What will they do now? The test has reached the crisis, and the brethren come through as men should. Not for a moment do they hesitate: '[Each man loaded his donkey] and returned to the city' (v. 13). Whether Benjamin was innocent or guilty, they were going to stand by him. Twenty years had wrought a welcome change in these men."

–Scroggie

Once again the brothers were before Joseph. Their falling on the ground before him (v. 14) was a token of penitence and perhaps a desire for forgiveness, as well as an unconscious fulfillment of his early dreams. How full are Judah's few words: "What shall we say to my lord? What shall we speak? Or how shall we clear ourselves? God has found out the iniquity of your servants; here we are, my lord's slaves, both we and he also with whom the cup was found" (v. 16). They sense that divine retribution has caught up with them. Rather than abandon Benjamin, all will go into servitude together. Again, Joseph tightens the screws in verse 17, telling the ten that they may return home, but that Benjamin must stay. It is at this point that Judah steps forward, but before we look at his eloquent words, something should be noted about Joseph and his cup.

Joseph's silver cup raises questions about him. Did he practice divination as the other Egyptians did, or was he simply continuing to act a part before his brethren? Divining among the pagans was done by attaching meanings to movements of liquids in a cup or to other chance configurations (see Ezekiel 21:21), or by a kind of crystal gazing. Such practices were alien to Israel, and as for Joseph, for him to practice this sort of thing would have been inconsistent with his words in 40:7–41:16. As for the words of verse 5, Charles C. Ryrie has suggested that it is unlikely that Joseph practiced divination. Rather, he believes this statement was made in order to emphasize the special significance of the cup. Joseph planned this situation in order to test his brothers. Either they would use this opportunity to get rid of Benjamin or else they would stick by him. Later in Israel's history God's people were forbidden to practice divination (Deut. 18:10-12).

Judah's Moving Plea (44:18-34)

Scroggie has commented that Joseph's words in verse 17 "acted upon Judah like a match to tinder; it was like the lifting up of a sluice-gate, releasing the flood in his soul.

> Judah's words have been described as "almost matchless in literature."

Here is artless art, the noblest eloquence, most moving pathos." Judah's words have been described as "almost matchless in literature," while Martin Luther said he would give anything if he could pray to God as Judah prayed to Joseph.

Let's consider now in some detail Judah's magnificent appeal, noting first of all *his simplicity and humility* (44:18-26). With beautiful simplicity, in keeping with humility he so genuinely exhibited in verse 18, Judah tells in the verses that follow the story of his aged father and the two sons of his wife. One is dead, while the other, whom he dearly loves, was born to him in later years and is the sole remaining child of his deceased wife (vv. 19-20). He then goes on in verses 21-26 to recount briefly the details of 43: 2-10.

A second thing to observe about Judah is *his sensitivity* (44:27-32). Here is the expression of real feeling on Judah's part. He tells Pharaoh of the other son born by Rachel, now presumed dead, and then of how Jacob's life is so bound up in young Benjamin (v. 30). Twice he informs "the one who is even as Pharaoh" (v. 18) that, if Benjamin should not return with them to his father, then his father's gray hair would be brought down to Sheol in sorrow (literally, evil). He further adds that he is surety (guarantee) for this brother, and that if he does not bring him back, then he is to bear the blame before his father forever (v. 32).

Finally, we see in Judah *his selflessness* (44:33-34). Judah asks that he might become a slave in place of his brother. It was a noble request, for he knew that Benjamin was preferred by Jacob to himself, and he was willing to even die in a foreign land for him. He would rather not return than to see his aged father die of a broken heart. Judah is not the man of Genesis 38. He is a changed man, and a man worthy to be the patriarch of Him who is the Lion of the tribe of Judah and the Lamb of God (see 49:8-10).

> The extremities and adversities of life often bring out true character or level of maturity in the individual.

Regarding the close of this stirring scene, Griffith Thomas said of Joseph's brothers, "At last they were united and were ready to suffer together."

POINTS TO PONDER

1. God pursued the ten brothers through Joseph's actions with a view to their repentance while they were still living.

2. Even if sin is not brought home to its perpetrators in this life, it will be in the next. We are clearly and firmly reminded in Hebrews 9:27 that "it is appointed for men to die once, but after this the judgment."

3. All sinners who die in their sins, having rejected Christ, will one day stand before God at His Great White Throne Judgment (see Revelation 20:11-15). In that day there will be no escape. The only present-day escape is to receive by faith the Lord Jesus Christ as your Savior, who offered Himself as the atoning sacrifice for our sins on the cross.

4. The extremities and adversities of life often bring out the true character or level of maturity of the individual. The humility and simplicity of Judah's appeal on behalf of Benjamin beautifully illustrates this (Gen. 44:18-26). _____ ❧ _____

5. God has built the principle of cause and effect, of sowing and reaping, into the moral fabric of human experience. This is a principle we cannot avoid. We are instructed in Galatians 6:7-8 to "not be deceived, God is not mocked; for whatever a man sows, that he will also reap. For he who sows to his flesh will of the flesh reap corruption, but he who sows to the Spirit will of the Spirit reap everlasting life."

> **God has built the principle of cause and effect, of sowing and reaping, into the moral fabric of human experience.**

6. We need to keep in mind that what God permits because of the action of others (1) may not be the fault of the individual in view; (2) can easily become the basis for bitterness; and (3) may never be understood in this life.

7. We must never commit a wrong to try and correct a wrong. In other words, two wrongs do not make a right. The teaching of God's Word is clear about this, the apostle Paul having written in Romans 12:19, "Beloved, do not avenge yourselves, but rather give place to wrath; for it is written, 'Vengeance is Mine, I will repay' says the Lord."

8. The sins of others do not give us an excuse to sin. The fact that others are committing a sin (or sins) and seemingly getting away with it does not give us a reason to follow their evil example.

9. We must not be "soft" on sin. Each of us needs to face up to his or her sins, including their spiritual and natural consequences, even though others may seem to get by with sin. Light (casual) views of sin lead to wrong views of God. Sin is a terrible and horrible offence to the living and true God. Remember, our sins occasioned the need for the Lord Jesus Christ to suffer, bleed, and die on the cross.

10. Let's not blame others for what we are individually responsible and accountable. It is the dismal habit of fallen humanity to generally blame someone else for our sins and failures. This is what Adam and Eve did in the Garden of Eden. When Adam sinned he blamed Eve, and when Eve was deceived and sinned she blamed the devil (Gen. 3:12-13).

> Let's not blame others for what we are individually responsible and accountable.

11. We must trust God when He allows trials to come into our lives. We have a wonderful promise in 1 Corinthians 10:13, that "no temptation has overtaken you except such as is common to man; but God is faithful, who will not allow you to be tempted beyond what you are able, but with the temptation will also make the way of escape, that you may be able to bear it."

CHAPTER

9

REVELATION, RESPONSE, AND REVIVING
(GENESIS 45:1-28)

At last there was no further need for Joseph to conceal his identity. He had learned what he wanted to know about his brothers, and now "the moment of truth" had arrived to reveal himself. And what a traumatic, emotion-packed moment it was!

Joseph Reveals His Identity (45:1-15)

Unable to control himself any longer because of the passionate eloquence of Judah in his appeal as mediator, Joseph requested that everyone leave the room except his brothers. So loud was his lamentation that the Egyptians and the house of Pharaoh heard it. Like a lightning bolt the words were blurted out from his mouth: "I am Joseph." The effect of his words are better imagined than described. Joseph's inquiry about his father were the words of love, not just courtesy. At any rate, his revelation of himself filled his brothers with considerable concern.

With considerate tenderness, Joseph said to his brothers, "Please come near to me" (v. 4). He then explained in choice theological sentiments the entire movement of events, from his sale as a slave to his present exalted position. The various details may be summed up in this way, "You sold me," but "God sent me" (v. 5 with vv. 7-8). Of every event there are two aspects: the human side and the divine side. And it is the latter side that is of real consequence. This truth has been beautifully demonstrated in the garden of Gethsemane. It was there that the Lord Jesus Christ accepted His destiny of dying on the cross as "the cup which My Father has given

Me" (John 18:11; cf. Gen. 50:20; Ps. 76:10; Acts 2:23-24; 4:28; 13:17; Rom. 8:28; Phil. 1:12).

The words, "to preserve a posterity for you in the earth, and to save your lives by a great deliverance" (v. 7), refer to the deliverance of the family from extinction. As Henry M. Morris has written, "Had this scene not occurred, the children of Israel would soon have scattered and merged with the other peoples of the Middle East—the Ishmaelites and Edomites and Canaanites." In essence, then, Joseph had been sold to be a slave, but God had sent him to be a savior.

————— ❧ —————

Joseph had been sold to be a slave, but God had sent him to be a savior.

————— ❧ —————

After Joseph set his brothers' minds at ease he commanded them to go and quickly bring Jacob and the family to Egypt (v. 9). Commenting on Joseph, W. Graham Scroggie wrote,

> "From the beginning he had thought of life in terms of God. He believed that every man's life is a plan of God, a plan that may easily be frustrated, but which also may be fulfilled. Joseph might well have written the words, 'Ill that He blesses is my good, and unblest good is ill, and all is right that seems most wrong, if it be His sweet will.'"

Someone has described verses 14 and 15 as "tear answering to tear." Joseph's kissing of his brothers served as the seal of reconciliation, a reconciliation brought about by the Lord and the agency of Joseph.

Notice the words, "after that his brothers talked with him" (v. 15). What did they talk about that day and probably into the night? After all, more than twenty years had elapsed; they had a lot to catch up on. Joseph undoubtedly related God's providential dealings with him, perhaps calling in his wife and two sons to introduce them to his brothers. In turn, Joseph's brothers would have told him about their families, further details about their father, and all else that had taken place over the years.

Pharaoh Responds and Provides (45:16-24)

The news of the presence of Joseph's brothers pleased both Pharaoh and his servants. It's obvious that Joseph was a widely esteemed Prime Minister. Not only was it known that Joseph was a former slave, but also that he was from an honorable family of free nomads, a class generally held in high esteem by the Egyptians of that day.

Such was Pharaoh's favor that he commanded Joseph to tell his brothers to load their beasts, go to Canaan, get Jacob, and return to Egypt. He promised them the best that Egypt could offer, and that they would "eat the fat of the land" (v. 18).

On verse 19, Barnhouse has written:

> "A wagon from Egypt was more rare in Palestine then than an airplane in the African bush today. It was most generous of Pharaoh to give the wagons and invite Jacob's family to leave their old possessions behind and receive the bounty of Egypt. Thus the king rewarded Joseph, who had done so much for him."

Later, when Jacob saw these bountiful provisions, they helped convince him of the truthfulness of the news that Joseph was still alive (v. 27).

The words of verse 20, "Also do not be concerned about your goods, for the best of all the land of Egypt is yours," have frequently been referred to as "the Old Testament equivalent of 'forgetting those things which are behind'" (Phil. 3:13). Our material possessions can often be an impediment in the Lord's service, and in our materialistic culture it is wise to ask ourselves just what part they play in our lives. As Barnhouse has further commented,

> **How many Christians have impeded their spiritual progress by clinging to their stuff!**

> "Whatever stuff you cling to can be only an impediment on your road to glory. This does not mean that you may not own a home, but the home must not own you. You may have money in the bank, but your true bank must be in heaven, not your heaven in a bank. How many Christians have impeded their spiritual progress by clinging to their stuff!"

Along with wagons and food for the journey, Joseph also gave them clothing; in addition, a gift was sent to Jacob. But as Scroggie has said, "All this was a small blessing in comparison with what they carried in their hearts—a sweet sense of forgiveness!"

Because Joseph knew human nature, he counseled his brothers not to quarrel on the trip home (v. 24), realizing that on a long journey they might start bickering among themselves as to who was really at fault for the wrong done to Joseph so many years before.

Jacob Revives (45:25-28)

As the "wagon train" approached the family home in Canaan, we cannot help but wonder just what was going through Jacob's mind as he glimpsed it in the distance. No doubt his first concern was to see Benjamin. As for his other sons, whatever their report might be it would be received with an element of suspicion.

Jacob is stunned by his sons' announcement that Joseph is not only alive but ruling over all the land of Egypt! At first he does not believe them. Can we blame him? After all, his sons had not exactly been known for their honesty in the past. However, they continued talking, "and when he saw the carts which Joseph had sent to carry him," we read, "the spirit of Jacob their father revived" (v. 27). It is a rather sad testimony to the past untruthfulness of his sons that Jacob had to see the wagons before he would believe them. Nevertheless, Joseph was alive. "What a story!" says Scroggie. And then he adds, "Yes, and *Jesus is risen from the dead!*"

Revived in spirit, Jacob is now ready to go down to Egypt. That was the human side of things. On the divine side, God had made things ready for the centuries in Egypt by which His people would be prepared for the further stages of His divine program.

Of this, and Joseph's revelation of himself to his brothers, Griffith Thomas has written:

> "It is a beautiful symbol of Christ's revelation to us: (1) Its method—love's privacy; (2) Its power—love's pardon; (3) Its fullness—love's peace; (4) Its assurance—love's provision. All that is needed is that this revelation of reconciliation should first be believed and then told to others."

POINTS TO PONDER

1. It's obvious that, over the years, Joseph held no grudges against his brothers for their cruel treatment of him. On the contrary, he possessed a loving, sensitive, and forgiving spirit.

2. Joseph accepted adverse conditions without self-pity. Feeling sorry for ourselves will only compound whatever harsh circumstances we may be experiencing.

——— ❧ ———

Feeling sorry for ourselves will only compound whatever harsh circumstances we may be experiencing.

——— ❧ ———

3. Joseph always thought of life in terms of God. He would have appreciated the statement, "God has planned out His work, and step by step He is working out His plan."

4. Pharaoh's kindness and generosity is a reminder that even in unlikely places there are benevolent people in positions of authority. Furthermore, the liberality Pharaoh was able to show after two years of famine (45:6) is a tribute to Joseph's outstanding wisdom, ability, and integrity.

5. When everything seems to be against us, life sometimes unfolds some pleasant surprises, as in the case of Jacob's experience. The key thing is to continually look to God to work things out according to His will, purpose, and timing.

6. King Solomon wrote, "As cold water to a weary soul, so is good news from a far country" (Prov. 25:25). The report to Jacob that Joseph was alive was indeed "good news from a far country"—the best he had received in years—and little wonder that Jacob's spirit "revived" (v. 27). Be patient, wait expectantly on God, and perhaps you too will receive some "good news" today which will revive your spirit.

10

A JOURNEY, A REUNION, AND AN INTRODUCTION
(GENESIS 46:1–47:31)

Circumstances, in and of themselves, are not always a clear guide to knowing the perfect will of God. Yet, here, through providential circumstances, it was evident to Jacob that it was indeed God's will for him to migrate to Egypt. After all, he was anxious to see Joseph, whom God had so wondrously preserved and exalted. Furthermore, to remain in Canaan would mean extreme poverty and probable death by starvation for both he and his family.

Nevertheless, Jacob was unsure. Had not his grandfather Abraham made an almost disastrous trip down to Egypt (Genesis 12)? And was not Canaan the very land God had promised to Abraham and Isaac? And could not God end the famine and miraculously meet their need right there in Canaan? Furthermore, until now, each time Jacob had taken an important step, God had spoken directly to him (cf. Genesis 28:13-15, at Bethel; 31:3, when he had been long enough with Laban; 35:1, when he left Shechem; and 35:9-12, from Padan Aram).

Thus it must have been with mixed emotions that the old patriarch prepared to leave Canaan. Nevertheless, with all that he had—family and servants, flocks and possessions—Jacob started for Egypt, every circumstance indicating that he should do so, and at the same time trusting God to block the way if this were not His clear will.

Jacob Journeys to Egypt (46:1-27)

Although on his way to Egypt, Jacob longed for some expression of divine encouragement regarding this giant step. Thus at Beersheba, Isaac's permanent home (see Genesis 26:23-25) and some twenty miles from Hebron, he humbly and worshipfully called on "the God of his father" (v. 1), thereby acknowledging the family calling and seeking divine approval of his move. Jacob's attitude was very different from that of Abram in Genesis 12:1. In response, God appeared to Jacob "in the visions of the night" (v. 2), the plural "visions" possibly referring to the various steps in the continuing encounter. Notice, Moses (the human author of Genesis) records that God spoke to "Israel" (i.e., Jacob) and said, "Jacob, Jacob." This may suggest that the message was to assure "Israel" about the future of the nation and "Jacob" of God's care for him personally.

God assures Jacob of His blessing upon his journey to Egypt, for "there" He would make of him a great nation (v. 3), these words going beyond the promises given to him at Bethel (35:11-12). In Egypt they would have all the advantages of the greatest nation on the earth at that time. There they would learn law and order, and they would be protected while they increased to a multitude. It was there that Moses would be born and ultimately lead them out of Egypt.

> ———— ❧ ————
> **Before decisions are made, God's will must be sought.**
> ———— ❧ ————

In verse 4 God assured Jacob of His abiding presence, this text serving as an illustration of the fact that believers should never move unless they are assured of His presence. Before decisions are made, God's will must be sought, else we shall move in vain. From this text we are reminded by Barnhouse that "our Lord is the God of the round trip. He never takes us partway. He carries us to our final destination. When He directs us to a dark place, it is for a great purpose."

The last clause of verse 4 is a reference to Joseph's closing of Jacob's eyes for him at death. Regarding these words, Barnhouse has touchingly commented that,

> "Many of us have kissed the brow of a loved one who has departed, and have tenderly closed the eyelids. If the Lord does not return to take us without dying, we shall long to have loved ones with us at the time of our exodus. To Jacob was given the promise that he would not die alone—Joseph's hand would close his eyes. This was a comfort to the aging patriarch."

Scroggie adds this insight:

> "What a journey that trip to Egypt was (vv. 5-7)! A family was about to become a nation; a nation which was destined to influence greatly the history of the whole world. Jacob was saying good-bye to Canaan for ever."

With reference to Jacob's family, some have imagined a discrepancy between verses 26 and 27. However, it must be observed that the register of family members who came out of Canaan with Jacob is arranged into its Leah and Rachel groups, and this gives a total of seventy. Adding Dinah (v. 15), but subtracting five other names (Er and Onan, buried in Canaan, v. 12; Joseph, Manasseh, and Ephraim, already in Egypt, v. 20) brings us to the actual number of sixty-six (v. 26). Verse 27 adds Joseph's two sons to Joseph and Jacob, and this gives the total of all of Jacob's house who had come to Egypt sooner or later in the account.

In the Bible the number seventy is significant, for it is the number of completeness. Moses chose seventy elders, and the Lord Jesus Christ, seventy disciples (cf. Luke 10:1).

Five other unnamed family members are mentioned in Acts 7:14, probably a reference to Joseph's grandsons, born in Egypt and mentioned in the Septuagint (the Greek translation of the Old Testament), which Stephen cited in his message before the Sanhedrin.

Jacob Is Reunited with Joseph (46:28-34)

We need never be ashamed of emotions; they are God-given, and are expressive of our humanity.

Verse 28 may either mean that Joseph was to be escorted by Judah to the family in Goshen or that Judah was sent to Joseph to find out from him where the family should settle in Goshen. Either explanation is satisfactory.

To be sure, the meeting of Jacob and Joseph is one of the most beautiful scenes of Scripture. Jacob was reunited with his beloved son, the firstborn of his beloved wife Rachel. The weeping continued for a long while with no words spoken. None were needed here. The sense of verse 30 is that Jacob can now die in peace. Here, the old patriarch expresses a note of satisfaction and hope (see 45:28). Through Moses the

Holy Spirit has recorded in these chapters numerous details of the emotions of various biblical characters. We need never be ashamed of emotions; they are God-given, and are expressive of our humanity. They are as much a part of us as the mind and the will.

In verses 31-34 Joseph wisely counseled his brothers that he would tell Pharaoh that they were shepherds. For some reason the Egyptians did not think well of shepherds. Therefore, he wisely told his brothers to frankly admit their occupation before Pharaoh. In this way, their separation in the land would be acceptable to Pharaoh and to the Hebrews. Joseph handled a difficult and delicate matter in a highly discreet manner.

Pharaoh Meets Joseph's Family (47:1-10)

Why were only five of Joseph's brothers brought before Pharaoh (v. 2)? We really don't know, other than the possibility that this number was significant among the Egyptians (see 43:34; 45:22). The Egyptians disliked shepherds, but Joseph had previously instructed his brothers to be open and above board with Pharaoh, and this is exactly what we should be if we are confronted with secular authorities. The honesty and frankness of Joseph's brothers paid off: Pharaoh gave them a plush area in which to live—the land of Goshen, a very fertile part of Egypt, with homes and property rights beyond those of the Egyptians themselves (vv. 5-6). Pharaoh's graciousness is seen here and elsewhere in the story of Joseph.

Notice that in the brothers' confession before Pharaoh that they had come to sojourn in the land of Egypt (v. 4), we have an unconscious fulfillment of the prophecy given to Abraham many years before (see Genesis 15:13-14).

At this meeting we might have thought that Pharaoh would have blessed Jacob. But, no, twice we read that Jacob, as God's representative, blessed Pharaoh (vv. 7 and 10). And we must not think of Jacob's blessing of Pharaoh as some kind of "may the king live forever" statement (see, for example, 2 Samuel 16:16). Rather, Jacob—a Hebrew saint—bestowed a heavenly blessing on Pharaoh—an Egyptian Sovereign—and the former is the greater figure (see Hebrews 7:7).

What did they talk about? Basically, they talked about the quantity and then the quality of life. Jacob evidently showed his age, for Pharaoh's first question was, "How old are you?" (v. 8). Apparently it was not common for a man to live 130 years in the pagan land of Egypt. Pharaoh's question led Jacob to speak of the brevity of life (our allotted days are not much over half of Jacob's at this point!)—"few and evil" had been his days, Jacob said. By this he meant that they had been short and sad. To be sure, Jacob's pilgrimage had been beset with many rough and jagged experiences.

"The 'evil' or unpleasantness of his [Jacob's] days is linked with the fact that as a young man he was forced to leave the association of his friends and home and spend some of the most important of his years as a stranger in a foreign land. He paid arduous and difficult service to Laban for his wives, the days consisting of experience with droughts, frosts, and other problems. He finally escaped the clutches of Laban only to fall into the path of Esau, who had threatened his life. At that moment he struggled with the Angel Wrestler and, while emerging victorious, he was left with a dislocated hip joint, upon which he limped to the end of his life. He was soon in difficulty with the Canaanites in Shechem through the folly of Levi and Simeon. He was forced to suffer the deaths of Deborah at Luz, and of his beloved Rachel at Ephrath. At Mamre he was given the task of burying his beloved father, Isaac. His son Joseph was lost to him for years. Reuben involved his name in reproach and disgrace, and Judah dragged the name of Israel through the mud of sexual sensualness. And, finally, he was forced to part with his last touch with Rachel, Benjamin, and make his way out of his beloved country down to the land of the pagans in Egypt. Yes, Jacob, your days, when looked at from the human perspective, do seem to have been 'evil' days."

–Johnson

In Genesis 48:15 and 16 we have the divine perspective of his life in Jacob's own words. Compared to Esau, one might think of Jacob as a failure, yet only Jacob—not Esau—could have blessed Pharaoh as he did, for he had truly come to know Jehovah and the wealth of spiritual blessing through all his afflictions that such knowledge brings. Despite all of Esau's worldly prosperity, it was Jacob alone who could bless Pharaoh with the blessings of God.

Joseph Administers His Policies (47:11-26)

By God's grace and providence, the Israelites were better off than the citizens of Egypt. In verses 11 and 12 we see that our faithful God does indeed lovingly care for His own. This is a valid and vivid teaching throughout the Scriptures, whether in the storms or the sunshine of life. God is faithful, and this is the certified testimony of His own right to this moment. And so shall He ever remain faithful.

Verses 13-26 actually follow the summary of 41:53-57, the narrative having been interrupted to accommodate the coming of Joseph's brothers and all the details and consequences involved in that event, as related in 42:1–47:12.

Someone has said that Romans 12:11 is a sort of summary of Joseph's life: "Not lagging in diligence, fervent in spirit, serving the Lord." He was certainly all of these. However, some have been critical of Joseph

> Our faithful God does indeed lovingly care for His own.

for too harsh a policy toward the Egyptians, particularly since all the property of the citizens ended up in Pharaoh's hands. Examine carefully, however, what Joseph did. He sold corn first for money, then for cattle, and then for labor. He nationalized the land and made the people tenant-farmers (not slaves), having asked them for only one-fifth of their produce as a rent. People in those days were expected to provide for themselves (a moral element missing in today's society) to the limit of their ability. It is noteworthy that they did not complain; instead, they said concerning Joseph, "You have saved our lives" (v. 25). Remembering that Joseph is a picture (type) of the Lord Jesus Christ, these words have *typical* significance, while the offer of the people to become Pharaoh's "slaves" reminds us that we, too, become the Lord's servants when we become believers in Christ (1 Thess. 1:9).

Observe that the priests' lands were not affected. Pharaoh probably overruled Joseph in the matter (v. 22). At any rate, the one true God was thoroughly vindicated at the time of the exodus (see Exodus 12:12).

Jacob Prepares to Die (47:27-31)

Jacob remained in Egypt for seventeen years and died when he was 147 years old. His final years were uneventful and peaceful. There is no hint of fear on Jacob's part as he approached death. As someone has put it, the man who fought with God and prevailed is not likely to be dismayed by engaging the king of terrors in struggle. Jacob's dying request of Joseph was, "Please do not bury me in Egypt" (v. 29). His request, other than a natural desire to be buried in the land of his origin, reveals his concern for the future of God's people and his faith in the Messianic promises which had been confirmed to him and to his fathers. Having obtained a promise from Joseph, supported by an oath, we read that the dying patriarch bowed in worship on the head of his bed (v. 31; see Hebrews 11:21).

What is your goal in life?

Throughout his frequently rough, jagged, thorny pilgrimage, Jacob had a goal—that of fellowship with God, with other believers, and with his fathers. While there were many times when he lost his way in pursuit of that goal, he found that ultimately he was honored by the living and true God and by the world (see Proverbs 22:29). In the end he stood before Pharaoh and gave a good witness. Furthermore, God has greatly honored Jacob, for even today the Lord speaks of Himself as "the God of Abraham, the God of Isaac, and the God of Jacob" (see Matthew 22:32).

What is your goal in life? Have you acknowledged your sins and by faith received Christ as your Savior and Lord?

POINTS TO PONDER

1. Through Jacob's words in Genesis 47:9, we are reminded that life for the believer is a "pilgrimage" (see Hebrews 11:13-14; 13:14 with 1 Peter 2:11). In other words, life has a starting point and a goal; every child of God should heed the admonition to set his or her affection "on things above, not on things on the earth" (Col. 3:2).

2. In Genesis 47, we have in Jacob a beautiful picture of what it means to die in faith. We all, sooner or later, face the fact of our own death (Hebrews 9:27). Jacob had to do this in his day, and in relation to this extremely important and deeply personal matter he has left us some helpful instruction.

3. In Joseph's brothers we have a commendable example of honest toil (Gen. 47:3-6).

4. There is illustrated in chapter 47 the sacredness of family life. Still another lesson is how God's people should deal with the temporal authority (see 1 Peter 2: 11-17).

5. Probably the most important lesson is exhibited in the supreme worth of God's saints.

Although our day is vastly different from Jacob's, the principles of God's purpose, guidance, and love remain the same. And we should seek to prove them in our daily lives, no matter what the difficulties may be.

11

JACOB'S BLESSING AND PROPHECY
(GENESIS 48:1–49:33)

What was Jacob's most remarkable act of faith? One might think that the answer is simple, immediately responding that it was his experience at Peniel, when he wrestled with the Angel of God. The answer to this is no. Then was it at Bethel, where he built an altar to God? No. Was it at Mahanaim, where he had the vision of angels? No. Where, then, do we find the answer? It is found in Hebrews 11:21 where, in describing Jacob's faith, it is written, "By faith Jacob, when he was dying, blessed each of the sons of Joseph, and worshiped, leaning on the top of his staff." It was evidently this act which had in it the quality of faith that marked out Jacob as one of God's faithful men, for it is this that is singled out by the Holy Spirit above all else in his experiences.

This incident is recorded in Genesis 48 and brings us to Jacob's deathbed, as well as to all the other details centering on this sacred scene, which is then followed by his remarkable prophecy in chapter 49.

Jacob Adopts Joseph's Sons (48:1-7)

A report came to Joseph that his father was "sick," the word conveying the idea of being worn down or infirm brought about by the effects of old age and disease. Recognizing that the end might be near, Joseph took his two sons, Manasseh and Ephraim, and went to Jacob's bedside to receive his blessing on his sons.

Stirred by the news that Joseph was coming, Jacob strengthened himself for the meeting (v. 2). On the human level there may have been kind admonitions by family members not to try and sit up, etc., but he probably sensed in his own soul that Joseph would be bringing his boys for their grandfather's blessing. At any rate, it seems that he was divinely enabled to move and sit by the side of his bed, leaning upon his staff. At least this is the picture conjured up both here and in Hebrews 11:21.

Once Joseph had arrived with his sons, Jacob—typical of old age—began to reminisce. He spoke of two places and two persons. The places are Bethel and Ephrath; the persons are God and Rachel. At Bethel, God appeared to Jacob, and at Ephrath, Rachel died.

> "Jacob has not much longer to live; now he turns his attention to the past. When life draws toward a close, a thousand things which have absorbed much of our time and strength will fade from our interest, if not from our memory, and only that will remain which has really held sway in the soul. . . . Should you at the end of life have time to reflect, what in your life do you suppose will stand out above all other things, promoting gratitude or regret? That will depend upon the things you are living for now."
>
> –Scroggie

In verse 5, Jacob speaks of Joseph's sons as "mine," and as Griffith Thomas has written,

> **The greatest legacy a man can leave his family is the legacy of a life lived in faith in the Lord Jesus Christ.**

"The adoption of Ephraim and Manasseh into the family of Jacob is very remarkable. They were thus separated from Egypt and its prospects as the sons of the prime minister, and included in the people of God. It must have been a real test for them."

What a beautiful picture of our adoption in Christ as sons of God (Gal. 4:4-5; Eph. 1:5; Rom. 8:15)! We don't fault men who think they have blessed their family when they leave them houses, lands, and other securities, but the greatest legacy a man can leave his family is the legacy of a life lived in faith in the Lord Jesus Christ and to bring them to Him for salvation by the effectual working of the Holy Spirit.

Jacob Blesses Joseph's Sons (48:8-20)

Whether because of the wanderings of his mind or because of his poor eyesight, Jacob asked regarding Joseph's two sons, "Who are these?" (v. 8).

Having learned their identity, perhaps for the second time, he warmly draws them to himself (vv. 8-10).

Bowing in filial respect (v. 12), Joseph placed his sons before Jacob in such a way as to make it easy for him to give Manasseh the firstborn's blessing (v. 13). But instead, Jacob, "crossing his hands" (NASB translation), gave the firstborn's blessing to the younger Ephraim (v. 14), and did this *knowingly.*

> "Genesis is marked by a passing-over of the first-born: Seth instead of Cain; Shem instead of Japheth; Abraham instead of Haran; Isaac instead of Ishmael; Jacob instead of Esau. Thus the sovereignty of the divine will is seen here as throughout Scripture. And so Joseph does not appear in the list of his father's sons, but instead, his own sons take his place."
>
> –Thomas

Joseph is the collective name for his two sons, and this is why in verse 15 it is stated that Jacob "blessed Joseph." In blessing him he blessed them, for Joseph was their representative and they were represented in him (see 1 Chronicles 5:1-2).

Someone has summarized Jacob's blessing of these men in a threefold way in verses 15 and 16, as he called upon the covenant God who *wills*, *works* and *wards* (see 28:13; 31:5, 42; 32:9; 46:3). The "Angel" (v. 16) is, of course, a reference to the pre-incarnate Christ (see 32:24, 28, 30).

> In these verses Jacob looks at life from both the human and divine standpoint. May our God help us always look at life in a similar way.

Possibly the idea (of God being a Shepherd) expressed in Psalm 23:1 arose out of verse 15. The reference to "all evil" in verse 16 reminds us of Jacob's words in 47:9, where he referred to his days as "few and evil." Thus in these verses Jacob looks at life from both the human and divine standpoint. How much better and wiser to look at life from the brighter standpoint of things. It's not unlike the difference between looking at the Rocky Mountains close up and then from a distance. In their proper perspective they are a thing of beauty. May our Lord help us always to look at life in a similar way.

Regarding Jacob, Scroggie has further noted:

"His life moves in an ellipse around the two places—Bethel and Peniel—the former witnessing his conversion, and the latter his consecration. Could he ever forget 'the Angel' (16), and could he impart a better blessing to these young men than, 'Let my name be named on them'—the name Israel, not Jacob? Observe the names of God (El) in all these names—Beth-el, house of God; Peni-el, face of God; Isra-el, prince of God. We may not have God's name in ours, but we may have His nature in ours."

Although it is clear from the text that Joseph was displeased by his father's giving the firstborn's blessing to the younger, the die was cast—this was what God had willed!

Jacob Blesses Joseph (48:21-22)

The pronoun "I" in verse 21 is emphatic in the Hebrew language here. Jacob knew he was about to die but, looking beyond men to God, he assured Joseph of God's abiding presence and of the fulfillment of His promises (v. 21). The words of verse 22 record something not disclosed elsewhere in Scripture. Regarding chapter 48 as a whole, Griffith Thomas sees in it a beautiful picture of godly old age and lists four things: (1) faith looking upward; (2) gratitude looking backward; (3) love looking outward; and (4) hope looking forward.

For all true believers, the best is yet to be!

Let's remember, for all true believers, *the best is yet to be!*

Jacob's Prophecy and Death (49:1-33)

Jacob's final words in chapter 49 are not so much a blessing on his sons as they are a prophecy of what his sons could expect in the future because of their individual characters and the various decisions they had made.

Some Bible scholars, like A. C. Gaebelein, see in Jacob's prophecy the entire history of Israel—past, present and future. Reuben, Simeon, and Levi personify the character of the nation up to the time of Christ.

Judah would be the royal tribe, since the Messiah (Shiloh, "the peace-bringer") would come from Judah, this pointing clearly to the period of time when Christ was on the earth. Zebulun and Issachar represent Israel scattered among the nations during this age of grace. Dan depicts apostate Israel during the future time of the Antichrist (the tribe of Dan is left out in Revelation 7).

Gad, Asher, and Naphtali picture the godly remnant of Israel during the Great Tribulation. Joseph personifies the second coming of Christ, while Benjamin, whose name means "son of the right hand," represents the thousand-year righteous reign of the King, the Lord Jesus Christ.

Most would agree that the final words of a dying man or woman are generally important and worth pondering. Certainly this is the case with Jacob. Pretend you are present on this solemn occasion listening to the last words of this stalwart patriarch.

His prophetic blessing looked forward to Israel's conquest and settlement in the land of Canaan. However, his words embrace not only the near future (Deut. 4:30; 31:29), but the distant future as well. Jacob's expression "in the last days" (Gen. 49:1) looks forward to a much more glorious age when Christ shall reign in righteousness for a thousand years (see Isaiah 2:2; Ezekiel 38:16).

Reuben (49:3-4) was Jacob's firstborn, although he does not address his other sons in their chronological birth order. In verse 3, Jacob praised Reuben. As the eldest he was entitled to a double inheritance. However, because of his sin of adultery (Gen. 35:22) and his unstable character, he would fail in leadership.

Simeon and *Levi* (49:5-7) were men of violence, anger, and cruelty, with disregard for both human beings and animals. Jacob had not forgotten their massacre and plunder at Shechem (Gen. 34:25). The consequences of their sin resulted in both tribes being scattered (v. 7). However, by God's grace, Levi became Israel's priestly tribe (Ex. 32:26; Joshua 21).

> Judah became Israel's dominant, kingly tribe from which came David, Solomon, and his ruling dynasty.

Judah (49:8-12) became Israel's dominant, kingly tribe from which came David, Solomon, and their ruling dynasty. Judah, whose name means "praise," would prevail over his enemies and be praised by his brothers. The details of these verses point forward to the coming of "the Lion of the tribe of Judah" (Rev. 5:5), the Lord Jesus Christ. "Shiloh" (v. 10) is a veiled reference to the promised Messiah. In a day to come He shall return and reign as "King of kings and Lord of lords" (Rev. 19:16). His kingdom will be characterized by paradise-like splendor and wealth with all the nations of the world subject to Him. The words of verses 10-12 assuredly anticipate this time.

Zebulun (49:13) was the tenth of Jacob's twelve sons; the sixth and last son of his wife Leah (Gen. 30:19-20; 35:23; 1 Chron. 2:1). Very little is said about him. His territory was actually landlocked, but he evidently benefitted from the important sea trade route that crossed his land.

Issachar (49:14-15) is likened to a strong donkey. However, the tribe's love of comfort and ease led them to becoming their enemy's slaves.

Dan (49:16-18), whose name means "judge," would carry out judgment in Israel, which his tribe did. Sadly, the tribe failed to maintain moral and spiritual faithfulness (Judges 13:2; 18:1ff.; 1 Kings 12:28-30; 2 Kings 10:29). He became characterized by treachery, like a poisonous snake by the roadside.

In verse 18, Jacob offers a tender prayer for the salvation of his people and himself.

Gad (49:19) ended up settling in an unprotected territory east of the Jordan River. Although subject to enemy attacks, it was predicted that Gad would triumph over his foes.

Asher (49:20) means "happy," the indication being that his tribe would settle in the rich, coastal, agricultural area north of Carmel. As a result he would provide rich food fit for royalty.

Naphtali (49:21) is likened to a doe (female deer) set free from confinement, speedily carrying good news. The tribe settled northwest of the Sea of Galilee.

Joseph (49:22-26) is likened to a vine that went over the wall separating Jews and Gentiles. He was shot at by his brethren, which often happens to those who are especially blessed by God. But God was with him, strengthened him, and extended his boundaries of blessing (v. 26). Joseph suffered, and his sons (Ephraim and Manasseh) were blessed by God. Reuben sinned, and his sons lost the blessing of God.

Benjamin (49:27) is given the promise and prophecy that he would become a victorious warrior tribe. It would appear that this small tribe was the most warlike of all the tribes, consistently conquering their foes and dividing the spoil. Both Sauls in the Bible were from this tribe: Israel's first king (1 Sam. 9:1, 2) and the apostle Paul (Phil. 3:5).

So ends this classic chapter. Jacob, who died 147 years old, requested that his body be buried alongside his wife Leah, in the same location as his father Isaac and grandfather Abraham. One might think that he would have requested to be buried alongside his beloved wife Rachel; the family heritage seems to hold the stronger ties.

If we must go through physical death as believers, it would be nice to die as Jacob did. When he finished his prophetic blessing, he simply drew his feet into the bed, breathed his last, and was gathered to his people.

POINTS TO PONDER

1. An inference we can make from the statement in Genesis 49:28 that Jacob "blessed each one" is the importance of treating people as individuals. This is a principle we see over and over again in the Bible. Certainly, *God* treats us as individuals.

2. The blessings/prophecies concerning each son differed widely, which reveals how well Jacob discerned the character traits and personalities of each of them. Jacob sets us an example in his final hours that we should take the time and trouble to "pay more attention to approaching death and prepare to leave our loved ones advice and admonition suited to their individual spiritual condition and progress." –Ken Fleming

3. In verse 2 Jacob appeals to his sons to hear and to listen to what he would tell them. The sons had an opportunity to listen to the words of their father Jacob and consider their character traits. We also need to listen to the words of our heavenly Father as He speaks to us and to allow His Word to change us.

4. "The restoration of the Levites to a position of service and worship reminds us that, like Paul, we can put our past behind us having 'obtained mercy' in Christ. He has given each of us areas of ministry and has enabled us to serve Him (1 Tim. 1:12-17). May He count *us* faithful too." –Ken Fleming

5. The life of Jacob reminds us that our lives will not be easy. There will be disappointments and failures. However we can learn from Jacob that we must keep pressing forward, accepting that which God brings into our lives, always aiming to please Him. "The triumphant end to Jacob's life should encourage all God's people to move on from the setbacks and disappointments of life. . . . Slowly over the course of his life God disciplined him to let go of his scheming, and he submitted himself increasingly to God." –Ken Fleming

12

FINISHING WELL
(GENESIS 50:1-26)

It is recorded of F. B. Meyer that he said to a friend, "I do hope my Father will let the river of my life go flowing fully until the finish. I don't want it to end in a swamp." And it was William Culbertson, one-time president of Moody Bible Institute, who was heard to pray toward the end of his life, "Lord, help us to end well!" Happily, Joseph's life didn't "end in a swamp." He went right on flowing fully to the end and finished well.

If it should be our experience to pass through physical death instead of leaving this world by way of the rapture (i.e., the return of Christ to the air for His church, see 1 Thessalonians 4: 13-18), how wonderful it is to die in the Lord. And what a difference it makes, both to the dying and to the loved ones who remain. To the former it means eternal life in all its fullness, while to the latter it means comfort and consolation.

> **How wonderful it is to die in the Lord.**

At least three things generally mark the death of a believer.

1. There is genuine faith in the promises of God, this certainly having been true of both Jacob and Joseph (Gen. 47:29-31; 49:29-32; 50:25; Heb. 11:22).

2. Alienations are generally absent. By this we mean that the atmosphere is one of love and harmony. In other words, any past strife, anger, bitterness, resentment, and so on, have been healed. This is illustrated in Jacob's death (Gen. 48:1-49:32), as well as Joseph's (Gen. 50:24).

3. The sure hope of reunion is usually one of the notes of a believer's final hours (Gen. 47:30), the classic New Testament statement of consolation regarding this theme being the apostle Paul's words in 1 Thessalonians 4:13-18.

As for the physical body of the believer, the Bible lays great stress on the *burial* of the faithful. There is no mention in Scripture of the practice of cremation, this being a pagan custom. While we believe that God is able to resurrect a cremated body, in the light of biblical teaching, it is clear that the body is important in the redemptive program (see 1 Corinthians 15:42 and following), and it is best that it be buried in the earth as the practices of the saints of Scripture indicate.

———— ❧ ————

The Bible lays great stress on the *burial* of the faithful.

———— ❧ ————

However, we must be careful to state that nowhere in the Bible is it indicated that it is wrong or sinful for a believer to have his or her physical body cremated.

Jacob's Burial (50:1-13)

Just as God had said, Joseph would have the task of closing Jacob's eyes in death (46:4). Jacob was 147 years old when he died, while Joseph at the time would have been about fifty-six.

At Joseph's command, his father's body was embalmed by Egypt's "physicians." Why did Joseph have this done? We really don't know, other than the fact that it was the one method available to preserve the body until it could be transferred to Canaan and buried there. Later, this would have been especially true in Joseph's case since his body was not brought up to the land of Canaan until hundreds of years after his death. At any rate, embalming served the providential purposes of God.

The Egyptians usually wept for a king for seventy-two days. It is noteworthy, then, that the Egyptians mourned for Jacob for seventy days. How true it is that God honors those who honor Him. Here was an aged Hebrew shepherd honored by a proud exclusive aristocracy of the ancient world, even though shepherds were an abomination to the Egyptians.

As we would have expected, Joseph's request of Pharaoh to travel to Canaan to bury his father's body was readily granted (vv. 4-6). Some have seen in the procession to Canaan (50:7-11) a rehearsal in miniature and in a minor key of the ultimate homecoming of the nation Israel to the land in a future day (see Isaiah 66:20). Jacob could easily have had an elaborate tomb in Egypt, but with good reason he preferred to be buried in "the cave of the field of Machpelah," where both Sarah and Abraham were buried (Gen. 23:7-9; 50:13).

Joseph Reassures His Brothers (50:14-21)

After Jacob's death, Joseph's brothers feared that he might seek revenge (v. 15). As is often the case, they evidently found it difficult to believe in the trustworthiness and nobility of one of God's true saints. Whether or not Jacob had really told Joseph's brothers that Joseph should forgive their transgression against him, is uncertain (vv. 16-17). Giving them the benefit of the doubt, we can assume that he did.

> Joseph's forgiveness is of a kind that reminds us of Christ's forgiveness; it is not of this world.

Joseph's response to the words of his brothers was no less than dramatic (vv. 17b-21). He wept. Whether his weeping reflected pity for their mistrust of him, or simply compassion over their concern and confession of sin, we cannot be sure. Perhaps both aspects were resident in Joseph's tears. At any rate, his forgiveness is of a kind that reminds us of Christ's forgiveness; it is not of this world.

Joseph Dies (50:22-26)

A period of fifty-four years lies between verses 21 and 22. As for Joseph, he experienced two great blessings. First, he lived to the age of 110, regarded in Egypt as an ideal age. Second, he saw his grandchildren (v. 23; see 48:11; Ps. 128:6).

Even the best and greatest of men must die (Heb. 9:27). However, before he left this world, Joseph had some last words. "I am dying," he said, "but God will surely visit you." His words reassured his loved ones of God's faithful presence. Still further, he promised that God will "bring you out of this land to the land of which He swore to Abraham, to Isaac, and to Jacob" (v. 24). Here, these words are the assurance of God's unfailing purpose. As part of his last words, Joseph requested that the sons of Israel swear to him that they would carry his bones up from Egypt to the land of Canaan. And this they did! (See Exodus 13:19; Acts 7:23, 25.)

Man has come from the Garden of Eden to a coffin in Egypt (v. 26). How sad if this were the end of God's dealings with man! However, Exodus—the book of redemption—follows, and so the Word of God goes on to assure every blood-bought child of God that a new and great day is coming which includes a new heavens and a new earth, a day wherein all of God's people will worship and serve Him throughout the ages to come.

Joseph's bones would have constantly reminded the children of Israel of a better day to come. Well, today we have no mummy case to remind us that the best is yet to be. We have something far better—the empty tomb! What assurance, comfort, joy, triumph, and blessing it speaks to the redeemed heart.

Have you come to the Lord Jesus Christ, who is the Resurrection and the Life, and received the forgiveness of sins and justification of life found alone in Him?

POINTS TO PONDER

From Joseph's interchange with his brothers in verses 17-21 we can glean three lines of Old and New Testament truth that we should receive by faith:

1. God is the ultimate Judge of all things. There is a day coming when all wrongs will be righted by Him, not by men (Rom. 12:19; 1 Thess. 5:15; 1 Peter 4:19).

> **God is the ultimate Judge of all things.**

2. God is the ultimate Governor of the universe. Although He is not the author of evil, God uses evil events in the process of carrying out His sovereign will and purposes (Gen. 45:5; John 18:11; Acts 2:22-24; 4:28; 13:27; Rom. 8:28, 29, 32, 38-39; Phil. 1:12).

3. Evil is to be repaid with forgiveness and love. Joseph personally promised his brothers that he would provide and care for them and their families. His words and the manner in which he promised them anticipate the teaching of the New Testament (e.g., Luke 6:27-38; Rom. 13:10; 1 John 3:16-18).

He Maketh No Mistake

My Father's way may twist and turn,
My heart may throb and ache;
But in my soul I'm glad I know,
He maketh no mistake.

My cherished plans may go astray,
My hopes may fade away;
But still I'll trust my Lord to lead,
For He doth know the way.

Tho' night be dark and it may seem
That day will never break;
I'll pin my faith, my all, in Him—
He maketh no mistake.

There's so much now I cannot see,
My eyesight's far too dim;
But come what may, I'll simply trust,
And leave it all to Him.

For by and by the mist will lift
And plain it all He'll make.
Through all the way, tho' dark to me,
He made not one mistake.

–A. M. Overton

BIBLIOGRAPHY

Atkinson, Basil F. C., *The Pocket Commentary of the Bible: The Book of Genesis*. Chicago, IL: Moody Press, 1957.

Barnhouse, Donald Grey, *Genesis: A Devotional Exposition*, Vol. 2. Grand Rapids, MI: Zondervan Publishing House, 1973.

Epp, Theodore H., *Joseph*. Lincoln, NE: Back to the Bible, 1971.

Fleming, Ken, *Genesis: From Creation to a Nation*. Dubuque, IA: ECS Ministries, 2005.

MacDonald, William, *Believer's Bible Commentary, Old Testament*. Nashville, TN: Thomas Nelson Publishers, 1992.

McGee, J. Vernon, *Thru the Bible with J. Vernon McGee*, Vol. 1. Nashville, TN: Thomas Nelson Publishers, 1981.

Morris, Henry M., *The Genesis Record*. San Diego, CA: Creation Life Publishers, 1976.

Pink, Arthur W., *Gleanings in Genesis*. Chicago, IL: Moody Press, 1922.

Thomas, W. H. Griffith, *Genesis: A Devotional Commentary*. Grand Rapids, MI: Eerdmans Publishing Company, 1946.

Thomas, W. H. Griffith, *Through the Pentateuch Chapter by Chapter*. Grand Rapids, MI: Eerdmans Publishing Company, 1957.

JOSEPH

A Life of Virtue

EXAM BOOKLET
AK '10 (1 UNIT) JOS

EXAM BOOKLET

STUDENT NAME (PLEASE PRINT)

ADDRESS

CITY, STATE, ZIP

COURSE GRADE: _____

INSTRUCTOR

Emmaus
CORRESPONDENCE SCHOOL

Exam developed by Emmaus Correspondence School, founded in 1942.

A NOTE ON THE EXAMS

The exams are designed to check your knowledge of the course material and the Scriptures. After you have studied a chapter, review the exam questions for that lesson. If you have difficulty in answering the questions, re-read the material. If questions contain a Scripture reference, you may use your Bible to help you answer them. If your instructor has provided a single page Answer Sheet, record your answer on that sheet. This exam contains the following types of questions:

MULTIPLE CHOICE

You will be asked to write in the letter of the correct answer at the space on the right. Here is an example:

The color of grass is

  A. blue.
  B. green.
  C. yellow.   **B**

WHAT DO YOU SAY?

These questions are designed to help you express your ideas and feelings. You may freely state your own opinions in answer to such questions.

RETURNING THE EXAM

See the back of this exam booklet for instructions on returning your exam for grading.

< DO NOT PHOTOCOPY THESE EXAM PAGES >

First Printed 2010 (AK '10), 1 UNIT
Reprinted 2012 (AK '10), 1 UNIT
Reprinted 2017 (AK '10), 1 UNIT

ISBN 978-1-59387-109-3

Code: JOS

Copyright © 2010 ECS Ministries

Printed in the United States of America

CHAPTER 1 EXAM

Joseph, Beloved and Hated

EXAM GRADE
_____

Before starting this exam, write your name and address on the front of this Exam Booklet. Read each question carefully and write the letter of the correct answer in the blank space on the right. Use the separate answer sheet if provided.

1. Of all the Hebrew characters in the Old Testament, one that best pictures Christ is

   A. Abraham.
   B. Jacob.
   C. Joseph.

   _____ C

2. We first meet Joseph when he was

   A. 16 years old.
   B. 17 years old.
   C. 21 years old.

   _____ B

3. Bilhah, who became one of Jacob's wives, was the mother of

   A. Simeon and Judah.
   B. Dan and Naphtali.
   C. Reuben and Issachar.

   _____ B

4. In Genesis 37 we learn that Joseph lived in

   A. Canaan.
   B. Mesopotamia.
   C. Moab.

   _____ A

5. Jacob gave Joseph a special

   A. sweater.
   B. pair of sandals.
   C. colorful coat (tunic).

   _____ C

6. Joseph was hated by his

   A. mother.
   B. brothers.
   C. father.

   _____ B

EXAM BOOKLET

7. In the dreams Joseph had, his brothers
   A. held a big party for him.
   B. bowed down to him.
   C. murdered him.   _C_

8. Joseph went to look for his brothers from his home at
   A. Jerusalem.
   B. Bethel.
   C. Hebron.   _C_

9. Joseph found his brothers at
   A. Dothan.
   B. Bethlehem.
   C. Beersheba.   _A_

10. When parents favor one of their children over another,
    A. it harms the family.
    B. it helps the family.
    C. it promotes healthy competition.   _A_

What Do You Say?

What in your background or upbringing has God given you grace to overcome?

A dissapointment /depression that brought about a aloneness to live.

CHAPTER 2 EXAM

SOLD INTO EGYPT

EXAM GRADE

Write the letter of the correct answer in the blank space on the right.
Use the separate answer sheet if provided.

1. When Joseph's brothers saw him coming, they referred to
   him as
   A. "that boy with the fancy coat."
   B. "Dad's favorite."
   C. "this dreamer."   *C*

2. Joseph's brothers planned to kill him and
   A. leave his body in a field.
   B. burn his body up.
   C. throw his body in a pit.   *C*

3. Joseph's life was spared at first by
   A. Judah.
   B. Simeon.
   C. Reuben.   *C*

4. While Joseph was in the pit, his brothers
   A. danced.
   B. sat down to eat.
   C. mocked him.   *B*

5. Joseph was sold to a caravan of
   A. Canaanites.
   B. Jebusites.
   C. Ishmaelites (Midianites).   *C*

6. Joseph was sold for
   A. 30 pieces of gold.
   B. 20 pieces of silver.
   C. 10 shekels.   *B*

7. Joseph's coat was stained by
   A. goat's blood.
   B. sheep's blood.
   C. his own blood.   *A*

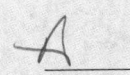

8. Joseph was resold in the land of

   A. Moab.
   B. Egypt.
   C. Edom.

B

9. Joseph was sold to

   A. Pharaoh.
   B. Potiphar's wife.
   C. Potiphar.

C

10. According to Genesis 37, Jacob mourned for Joseph

   A. many days.
   B. six weeks.
   C. one month.

A

WHAT DO YOU SAY?

The author says, "Somewhere along the line, our words and actions will . . . influence . . . others for good or evil." How have you personally experienced this principle?

I've seen my words influence for good when I've from time mentoring others on the principles I've learned over life's years. I've also seen my words influence people negatively when I've made a comment and it's received in a negative way, and the attitude and disposition of the person changed towards me.

CHAPTER 3 EXAM

TRIAL AND TRIUMPH

EXAM GRADE
_____

Write the letter of the correct answer in the blank space on the right.
Use the separate answer sheet if provided.

1. Potiphar was
   A. Pharaoh's treasurer.
   B. Pharaoh's bodyguard.
   C. captain of Pharaoh's bodyguards.   *C*

2. Potiphar
   A. ignored Joseph.
   B. persecuted Joseph.
   C. favored Joseph.   *C*

3. Joseph was
   A. handsome.
   B. unattractive.
   C. homely.   *A*

4. Joseph was tempted by
   A. Potiphar's sister.
   B. Potiphar's wife.
   C. a female prison attendant.   *B*

5. When faced with sexual temptation, Joseph
   A. ignored it.
   B. entertained it.
   C. fled from it.   *C*

6. Joseph was falsely accused on the evidence of his
   A. clothing.
   B. sandals.
   C. ring.   *A*

7. Temptation becomes a sin when we
   A. experience it.
   B. yield to it.
   C. entertain it.   *B*

EXAM BOOKLET

8. In Potiphar's house and in the prison, Joseph was
   A. completely trusted.
   B. under suspicion.
   C. treated with contempt.   _A_

9. Joseph was strengthened and encouraged by the fact that
   God was
   A. with him most of the time.
   B. with him all of the time.
   C. with him some of the time.   _B_

10. *We* can best resist Satan by
    A. our own strength.
    B. relying on Christian friends.
    C. obeying the Word of God (the Scriptures).   _C_

WHAT DO YOU SAY?

Read the final paragraph of the lesson again on pages 23 & 24. Pick one or two of the steps listed there and share how they are helping you resist temptation.

To read, study, memorize, meditate, and obey the
Word helps also in our living temptations. As
well as spending time in prayer, when I
spend time in prayer I offer myself to the Lord
in submission, and it gives me the strength
through the reading of the Word to resist
the temptations, and the enemy flees as I
consistent in those steps

CHAPTER 4 EXAM

DIVINE DISCIPLINE IN PHARAOH'S DUNGEON

EXAM GRADE
_____

Write the letter of the correct answer in the blank space on the right.
Use the separate answer sheet if provided.

1. Joseph's prison experience
   A. made him bitter.
   B. caused him to become withdrawn.
   C. prepared him for the future.   *C*

2. The chief cupbearer was responsible for Pharaoh's
   A. water supply.
   B. wines.
   C. pots and pans.   *B*

3. To learn God's will in our time
   A. we should learn how to interpret our dreams.
   B. we should read the Bible.
   C. we should listen to Bible scholars.   *B*

4. In prison, the chief cupbearer and chief baker experienced
   A. dreams.
   B. hallucinations.
   C. nightmares.   *A*

5. Joseph's ability to interpret dreams was
   A. self-taught.
   B. God-given.
   C. learned from the Egyptians.   *B*

6. In his interpretation of the cupbearer's and baker's
   dreams, Joseph
   A. withheld the truth.
   B. told the truth.
   C. watered down the truth.   *B*

7. The chief cupbearer was
   A. kept in prison.
   B. hanged.
   C. restored to his position.   *C*

E 9

8. The chief baker was

   A. restored to his position.
   B. kept in prison.
   C. hanged.

   _C_

9. When the cupbearer was released from prison,

   A. he forgot Joseph.
   B. he remembered Joseph.
   C. he had Joseph released.

   _A_

10. Joseph's interpretation of dreams was

    A. totally accurate.
    B. partly accurate.
    C. greatly flawed.

    _A_

WHAT DO YOU SAY?

How have your own experiences and trials been the means of developing your Christian character?

It is as was in the last paragraph. It's all been assigned by the divine hand of God, and in the midst of it I've learned to trust and depend totally on the Lord for his timing & grace for my deliverance. I've learned in quietness and trust is my strength.

CHAPTER 5 EXAM

FROM PRISON TO PRIME MINISTER

EXAM GRADE _____

Write the letter of the correct answer in the blank space on the right.
Use the separate answer sheet if provided.

1. Joseph remained in prison for another
   A. year.
   B. two years.
   C. six months.
    B

2. Pharaoh's first dream was of
   A. cows.
   B. horses.
   C. sheep.
    A

3. Pharaoh's second dream was of
   A. fish.
   B. cattle.
   C. ears of grain.
    C

4. Joseph was finally remembered by the
   A. baker.
   B. cupbearer.
   C. palace magicians.
    *B*

5. At this time Joseph was
   A. 21 years old.
   B. 30 years old.
   C. 26 years old.
    B

6. Before going in to meet Pharaoh, Joseph
   A. shaved his head.
   B. bathed in the Nile River.
   C. fasted for two days.
    A

7. Pharaoh chose Joseph to be his
   A. prime minister (second only to Pharaoh).
   B. secretary.
   C. personal bodyguard.
    A

EXAM BOOKLET

8. Joseph's wife's name was
   A. Asahel.
   B. Asenath.
   C. Asahiah.

   B

9. Joseph's two sons were named
   A. Manahath and Ephratah.
   B. Manocho and Ephrath.
   C. Manasseh and Ephraim.

   C

10. Joseph predicted a future famine of
    A. two years.
    B. five years.
    C. seven years.

    C

WHAT DO YOU SAY?

Give an example of God's faithfulness to you in an area you have exercised trust in Him.

So many examples come to mind, so there was a first. True my landlord sent a letter to say my rent would be raised by $400. I was panicked, I started to frantically look around for apartment, and none was available, and I had a "sister" in the church who taught it was her time for praying games... In the midst of hopeless ness I turned to the scripture and reminded my self the promise not to worry for our father knows what I need. I returned the letter to landlord and true stated I'll be leaving within the 60 day notice. They could break and said true rent increase was not for me. They wanted me to stay in the apartment, so disregard the letter.

CHAPTER 6 EXAM

THE GOADING OF A GUILTY CONSCIENCE

_____
EXAM GRADE

Write the letter of the correct answer in the blank space on the right.
Use the separate answer sheet if provided.

1. The period of time between Genesis 37 and chapter 42
    was at least

    A. 20 years.
    B. 26 years.
    C. 30 years.

    A

2. There can be no real repentance of sins apart from

    A. a sense of well-being.
    B. a sense of forgetting the past.
    C. a sense of guilt.

    C

3. Joseph's brothers journeyed from Canaan to Egypt
    because in Canaan there was

    A. political unrest.
    B. famine.
    C. war.

    B

4. Joseph's brothers went to Egypt minus their brother

    A. Benjamin.
    B. Simeon.
    C. Judah.

    A

5. When Joseph's brothers were brought before him in
    Egypt, they

    A. thought they recognized him.
    B. did not recognize him.
    C. recognized him.

    B

6. At first Joseph treated his brothers

    A. roughly.
    B. kindly.
    C. indifferently.

    A

EXAM BOOKLET

7. Joseph put his brothers in prison for

   A. three months.
   B. three days.
   C. three weeks.

   B

8. Joseph sent his brothers back to Canaan minus

   A. Reuben.
   B. Judah.
   C. Simeon.

   C

9. When they returned to Canaan and opened their sacks, Joseph's brothers discovered

   A. money.
   B. gold.
   C. jewels.

   A

10. Jacob's reaction to his circumstances generated by his sons was one of

    A. despair.
    B. joy.
    C. anger.

    A

What Do You Say?

How has God worked through your conscience to bring you to an awareness of sin in your life?

_____

_____

_____

_____

CHAPTER 7 EXAM

FRUSTRATION, FEAR, AND FAVOR

_____
EXAM GRADE

Write the letter of the correct answer in the blank space on the right.
Use the separate answer sheet if provided.

1. A second trip to Egypt by Joseph's brothers was necessary
   in order to
   A. see Simeon.
   B. report to Pharaoh.
   C. buy more food.   _____

2. At first, Jacob was not willing to send to Egypt his
   youngest son
   A. Asher.
   B. Benjamin.
   C. Gad.   _____

3. Jacob was finally convinced against his will by
   A. Judah.
   B. Issachar.
   C. Naphtali.   _____

4. Another name in Genesis 43 by which Jacob is called is
   A. Joshua.
   B. Ishmael.
   C. Israel.   _____

5. When Joseph's brothers arrived again in Egypt, they were
   taken to
   A. Pharaoh's palace.
   B. Potiphar's house.
   C. Joseph's house.   _____

6. Joseph's brothers tried first to explain about the money
   found in their sacks to
   A. Joseph.
   B. Joseph's steward.
   C. Potiphar.   _____

7. Joseph's brothers fulfilled the dream recorded in Genesis
   37:7-11 by
   A. visiting Joseph in Egypt.
   B. bringing Benjamin to Joseph.
   C. bowing down to Joseph.   _____

8. Egyptians looked upon foreigners as
   A. equal with them.
   B. unclean.
   C. friends.   _____

9. Joseph seated his brothers in his house according to their
   A. height.
   B. treatment of him.
   C. age.   _____

10. The author says that Joseph's love for Benjamin is a
    picture of
    A. the Lord's love for His people.
    B. Moses' love for Israel.
    C. Judah's love for Jacob.   _____

What Do You Say?

The author says, "God often uses the moral power of the fear of judgment
to prove, search, guide, warn, and purify us." Comment on this from your
own life.

_____

_____

_____

_____

CHAPTER 8 EXAM

JOSEPH AND JUDAH

_____
EXAM GRADE

*Write the letter of the correct answer in the blank space on the right.
Use the separate answer sheet if provided.*

1. Joseph's silver cup was placed by his steward in
   A. Judah's sack.
   B. Benjamin's sack.
   C. Simeon's sack.   _____

2. Joseph's unusual treatment of his brothers was to
   A. tease them.
   B. antagonize them.
   C. test them.   _____

3. Accused of theft, Joseph's brothers chose to
   A. return home.
   B. return to Egypt.
   C. stay where they were.   _____

4. When the brothers were brought again before Joseph, they
   A. fell down before him.
   B. protested their innocence.
   C. offered to pay a fine.   _____

5. When the brothers were brought again before Joseph, they
   were told they could go but that
   A. Simeon must stay.
   B. Reuben must stay.
   C. Benjamin must stay.   _____

6. At this point in the account, the spokesman for Joseph's
   brothers was
   A. Judah.
   B. Benjamin.
   C. Simeon.   _____

EXAM BOOKLET

7. The appeal that the brothers' spokesman made was
   A. arrogant and demanding.
   B. humble, sensitive, and simple.
   C. awkward and hesitant.   _____

8. Judah's selflessness was displayed when he told Joseph he
   was surety (a guarantee) for
   A. his brothers.
   B. their possessions.
   C. Benjamin.   _____

9. The author suggests that at the close of the scene in
   Genesis 44, Joseph's brothers were
   A. unresponsive.
   B. united.
   C. divided.   _____

10. Which of these NT verses relates to God's faithfulness to
    help us endure the trials of life?
    A. 1 Corinthians 10:13
    B. Romans 8:31
    C. 1 Thessalonians 4:7   _____

WHAT DO YOU SAY?

Comment on one of the "Points to Ponder" that speaks especially to you.

_____

_____

_____

_____

CHAPTER 9 EXAM

REVELATION, RESPONSE, AND REVIVING

EXAM GRADE
_____

Write the letter of the correct answer in the blank space on the right.
Use the separate answer sheet if provided.

1. Before Joseph revealed his identity, he requested
   A. Pharaoh's presence.
   B. Everyone to leave except his brothers.
   C. Potiphar's presence.

2. Joseph's emotional response was
   A. subdued.
   B. cold.
   C. loud with crying.

3. Joseph's first inquiry of his brothers was for
   A. conditions at home.
   B. his father.
   C. the welfare of the flocks at home.

4. Upon revealing himself, Joseph said to his brothers
   A. "Come near to me."
   B. "Now leave me alone."
   C. "Go home and don't come back."

5. Joseph thought of every man's life in terms of
   A. mere chance.
   B. good or bad luck.
   C. God's planning.

6. The news of the presence of Joseph's brothers
   A. shocked Pharaoh.
   B. displeased Pharaoh's servants.
   C. pleased Pharaoh and his servants.

7. Pharaoh wanted Joseph's family to
   A. remain in Canaan.
   B. come to Egypt.
   C. settle in a nearby wilderness.

EXAM BOOKLET

8. In those days, wagons from Egypt were

   A. rarely seen in Canaan.
   B. often seen in Canaan.
   C. first developed by the Canaanites.   _____

9. The greatest thing Joseph's brothers carried back to
   Canaan was

   A. their possessions.
   B. a gift for their father from Pharaoh.
   C. a sweet sense of forgiveness.   _____

10. When Jacob's sons returned home, he at first

   A. would not receive them.
   B. fainted at their report.
   C. did not believe their word about Joseph.   _____

WHAT DO YOU SAY?

What lessons have you learned from this portion that you can put into
practice this week?

_____

_____

_____

_____

CHAPTER 10 EXAM

A JOURNEY, A REUNION, AND AN INTRODUCTION

EXAM GRADE
_____

Write the letter of the correct answer in the blank space on the right.
Use the separate answer sheet if provided.

1. Circumstances are a clear guide to knowing God's will
   A. at all times.
   B. sometimes.
   C. at no time.   _____

2. Jacob left Canaan for Egypt with
   A. mixed emotions.
   B. absolute certainty.
   C. no assurance at all.   _____

3. On his way to Egypt, Jacob called on the name of the
   Lord at
   A. Bethlehem.
   B. Bethel.
   C. Beersheba.   _____

4. Jacob's departure from Canaan was for
   A. six months.
   B. six years.
   C. the last time.   _____

5. The actual number of family members who left Canaan
   with Jacob numbered
   A. 66.
   B. 69.
   C. 72.   _____

6. The register of family members who came out of Canaan
   with Jacob was arranged into its
   A. Leah and Rachel groups.
   B. Ephraim and Manasseh groups.
   C. Jacob and Esau groups.   _____

7. In the Bible, seventy is the number of

   A. incompleteness.
   B. assurance.
   C. completeness.   _____

8. Jacob's family settled in

   A. Thebes.
   B. Goshen.
   C. Memphis.   _____

9. For some reason the Egyptians did not think well of

   A. shepherds.
   B. tent dwellers.
   C. farmers.   _____

10. When Joseph was faced with telling Pharaoh the
    occupation of his brothers,

    A. he told the truth.
    B. he covered up the truth.
    C. he compromised the truth.   _____

WHAT DO YOU SAY?

Recognizing that "we became the Lord's servants when we believed in Christ," how are you currently serving the Lord?

_____

_____

_____

_____

CHAPTER 11 EXAM

JACOB'S BLESSING AND PROPHECY

EXAM GRADE

Write the letter of the correct answer in the blank space on the right. Use the separate answer sheet if provided.

1. Hebrews 11:21 reads, "By faith Jacob, when he was dying, _____ and worshipped, leaning on the top of his staff."
   A. blessed each of his sons
   B. blessed each of the sons of Joseph
   C. retold his life's history

2. The best kind of legacy a man can leave his children is
   A. traditions for the family line to keep.
   B. a material or financial one.
   C. a testimony of having lived for Christ.

3. Jacob gave the traditional blessing of the firstborn son to
   A. Manasseh.
   B. Ephraim.
   C. neither, as their mother was not a Hebrew.

4. What Jacob said about God in Genesis 48:21 reveals
   A. his naivety.
   B. his presumption.
   C. his faith.

5. Jacob's "blessing" of his twelve sons can be better termed
   A. prophecy.
   B. teaching.
   C. encouragement.

6. The son whose tribe eventually became Israel's leading and kingly tribe was
   A. Reuben.
   B. Joseph.
   C. Judah.

EXAM BOOKLET

7. Jacob requested that he be buried
   A. alongside his favorite wife, Rachel.
   B. in the family grave in Canaan.
   C. in Egypt. _____

8. When he died, Jacob was
   A. 147 years old.
   B. 143 years old.
   C. 137 years old. _____

9. One example Jacob sets us in relation to preparing for death is
   A. having something appropriate to say to our loved ones.
   B. making a will.
   C. making our own burial arrangements. _____

10. The tribe of Levi's eventual elevation to serve as Israel's priesthood reveals
    A. God loved Levi and hated Simeon.
    B. God forgot Levi's sin at Shechem.
    C. God's grace and mercy. _____

WHAT DO YOU SAY?

Read again the quote from Scroggie on page 72. How would you respond to his challenge? What do you expect "will stand out above all other things, promoting gratitude or regret" at the end of your life?

_____

_____

_____

_____

CHAPTER 12 EXAM

Finishing Well

<u>EXAM GRADE</u>

Write the letter of the correct answer in the blank space on the right. Use the separate answer sheet if provided.

1. The author suggests that cremation of a dead physical body was
   A. a Bible custom.
   B. a pagan custom.
   C. an Egyptian custom.

2. Jacob's body was
   A. cremated by the Egyptians.
   B. embalmed by the Egyptians.
   C. buried by the Egyptians.

3. Jacob was mourned by the Egyptians for
   A. 40 days.
   B. 70 days.
   C. 72 days.

4. Jacob's body was taken to Canaan and placed in the
   A. cave of Machpelah.
   B. cave of Adullam.
   C. cave of Makkedah.

5. After Jacob's death, Joseph's brothers feared that Joseph might
   A. forsake them.
   B. seek revenge.
   C. send them back to Canaan.

6. When Joseph learned what his brothers were thinking,
   A. he wept.
   B. he laughed.
   C. he was angry.

7. Following Jacob's death, Joseph lived in Egypt at least
   another
   A. 44 years.
   B. 46 years.
   C. 54 years.   _____

8. When he died, Joseph was
   A. 110 years old.
   B. 115 years old.
   C. 147 years old.   _____

9. Before he died, Joseph assured his brothers that God
   would
   A. keep them in Egypt.
   B. take them out of Egypt.
   C. enable them to conquer Egypt.   _____

10. Joseph made his brothers promise that ultimately they
    would
    A. bury his bones in Egypt.
    B. scatter his bones in the desert.
    C. carry his bones to Canaan.   _____

WHAT DO YOU SAY?

What is your attitude towards your own eventual passing? How has this
lesson helped you on this subject?

_____

_____

_____

_____

RETURNING THE EXAM BOOKLET FOR GRADING

✓ After completing all the exams, check them carefully.

✓ <u>Carefully</u> tear out the exam pages along the perforation provided near the book spine.

✓ Make sure you have followed all directions.

✓ Be sure you have written your correct name and address on all material you will send to the School.

✓ Return all the exams at one time instead of separating and mailing each individual exam.

✓ Return only the exam section, not the entire course book. If you have used the Single Page Answer Sheet, return only that sheet.

✓ Address the envelope correctly.

✓ Put the correct postage on the envelope.

✓ If you are studying this course through an Associate Instructor or associated ministry or organization, send the exams to the individual or organization from which you obtained the course. Otherwise, send them to the address below.

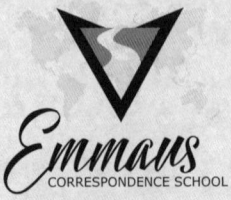

Emmaus Correspondence School
(A Division of ECS Ministries)
PO Box 1028
Dubuque, Iowa 52004-1028
phone: (563) 585-2070
email: ecsorders@emmauscourses.org
website: www.emmauscourses.org